The You-Don't-Need-
A-Man-To-Fix-It Book

The You-Don't-Need-A-Man-To-Fix-It Book

The Woman's Guide to Confident Home Repair

Jim Webb & Bart Houseman

Introduction By Erma Bombeck

DOUBLEDAY & COMPANY, INC.
GARDEN CITY, NEW YORK

To the Goucher alumnae of "Nuts and Bolts in Contemporary Society" who, by their own determination, turned themselves into handywomen.

Contents

Introduction

This is an introduction to a book that asks the question, "Did you marry for love or did you marry just to get your toilet fixed?"

That is ridiculous. There is no separating the two. Love is living in a house where there is a light in the hallway. Love is a man who can use a plunger without having to stand on it. Love is having a doorbell that doesn't have a sign on the door that reads, BREAK GLASS IN CASE OF EMERGENCY.

To be honest, for years women have succumbed to the myth that husbands are handy. To have one who was not handy was like admitting he didn't watch football games, use an anti-perspirant, or read *Playboy* at the barber shop.

I didn't expect my husband to read a steam-iron warranty manual on our honeymoon, but when we checked into the motel I began to suspect he was less than "handy" when he asked, "Where is the . . . what do you call those little devils all over the walls?"

"Light switches?" I asked slowly.

"That's it." He grinned. "Light switches. Got to remember."

"And that big round thing up in the ceiling is called a light," I said.

"Not too much knowledge in one day," he cautioned. "I've got to pace myself."

During the early years of our marriage, I think he really

tried. He fixed our toaster. It didn't work, but the garage door began to go up and down and it wasn't even electric.

He shaved a door that was too long and the dog ran under it and we never saw him again.

He inserted a towel rack in our living room because the wall already had holes from the previous tenants.

He sunk a clothes post for me and the neighborhood was without gas for thirty-six hours.

Things came to a head one Christmas Eve when the children were in bed and we were in the middle of the floor with a dismantled tricycle.

I sat by helplessly while he ran back and forth to the garage trying one tool and then another. Finally, he sat back and sighed. "It's no use. I'll have to go next door and ask Paul if he can help."

"To open the box?"

He shrugged his shoulders. "If this was a bubbling toilet, I'd know exactly what to do."

"What would you do?" I asked curiously.

"I'd call a plumber."

Three hours later my husband had assembled a tricycle with two wheels in the front, one in the back, an armrest on the handlebars, and a seat with a pedal on it two inches off the ground. "I have three wing nuts and a fender left over," he said joyously.

I began to ask myself, "Can a nice girl who is used to hot water, appliances and a dry basement find happiness with a klutz?"

Can a woman bear children for a man who considers electricity a fad like the Hula-Hoop and wedgies?

I answered myself, "No way."

"Something has to give," I told him one day. "We are the sole support of a plumber in Palm Beach, an electrician wintering in Cannes, and a Roto Rooter man who is retiring at twenty-three. What do you think the answer is?"

"I think it is time you became liberated," he said.

"And how am I supposed to do that?"

"I will pass on to you all that I have learned through my years of handymaning. Some things you will want to write down . . . others, I think you can remember. First, this is my toolbox. If you want to take a moment to familiarize yourself . . ."

I opened a small fishing tackle box that had FIRST AID crossed out on the front and TOOLS printed above it. Inside was a cork, five feet of pink plastic clothesline, a screwdriver with paint on the end, a small hammer, a safety pin, and a flashlight with no batteries.

It was like being sent to war armed only with long fingernails.

"Now, there are a few things I have discovered through trial and error that might be helpful to you," he began. "First, do not stand in the snow in your bedroom slippers and test Christmas tree lights. Second, do not stick your head down the vacuum sweeper bag and turn it on to see if it is 'sucking' properly. Third, you cannot seal leaky plumbing with the children's modeling clay. Fourth, there are easier ways to find the stud in the walls than to drill a line of holes and insert barbecue skewers until they hit something. That is all I know. Good luck."

For the past several years I have been coping with my newfound freedom as best as I could. Some things, of course, I could not fix. I have been writing columns and novels without the use of the letter *s* which sticks on my typewriter. (No wonder I never made it big. Who wants to read a book without ex?) I have been cooking on a stove with a timer that buzzes all the time the meal cooks but stops when the meal is done. I have been riding in a car with the glove compartment in my lap. And I must remember to kick the bed three times if I want the record changer to change automatically.

Just when it seemed our marriage had reached its highest

tolerance of inconvenience, I received a copy of *The You-Don't-Need-A-Man-To-Fix-It Book* in the mail. The authors, Jim Webb and Bart Houseman, caught my attention with such provocative questions as "Does your doorbell work only on Halloween? Do you have a window so hard to open that you painted the crowbar green to match the curtains? Do you blush when the hardware salesman asks if you want a male or a female plug?"

The You-Don't-Need-A-Man-To-Fix-It Book won't turn you into a licensed plumber or an electrician, nor does it mean to. All it is saying is that the push-button world we live in has several marked p-a-n-i-c and that if you have a little information and know-how you can readily get things to working again without the expense and the bother of a repairman. It has taken into consideration that it is *women* who are stuck with the inconveniences, and the odds are pretty good that it is *women* who will have to solve these problems.

This book will not only do a lot for the marriages of this country, it might even save a single girl from an early one. There's a lot to be said for a liberated handywoman and the authors have said it well.

Whatever your status, *The You-Don't-Need-A-Man-To-Fix-It Book* makes the Miss, Mrs., or Ms. less miserable.

Note to the reader:
This book has two authors, but it seemed awkward to use the pronoun "we." So we used "I."

JIM WEBB AND BART HOUSEMAN

The You-Don't-Need-
A-Man-To-Fix-It Book

1

Who Said That Women Have to Be Helpless?

It's as American as PTA and power steering, and it begins innocently enough in the jolly name of Santa Claus.

Every year under any one of a million Christmas trees, a tiny tool chest waits for Bobby while a doll carriage lies ready for Bobbi. Joe will unwrap a radio kit, but Jo will get a tea set.

It's unfortunate, but true, that the same conscientious father who patiently teaches his son how to straighten a bent nail tells his daughter to "get out of the workshop before you hurt yourself," and the same mother who feels that both her son and her daughter should wash dishes expects only her son to know how to adjust the lawn mower. The same school that requires every boy to learn to use a saw allows girls to consider such skills superfluous.

The young woman emerging from high school finds that, while her male counterpart is encouraged to try engineering or medicine, she is encouraged to take up decorating, dressmaking, and découpage. And, if she decides to marry, her friends shower her with a lifetime supply of measuring cups, but not a single wrench or hammer.

A rental agreement or a house mortgage later, the American Ms. wakes up to find herself the manager of a mechanically complicated home or apartment complete with ailing gadgets, hissing toilets, squeaky floors, and silent doorbell. Maybe even equipped with a male who is, by assumption, properly prepared and eminently eager to cure every little mechanical problem.

I remember a college woman who assured me that, although she herself knew as much about tools as does the average Indian princess, her problems would only be little ones, because she was marrying Roger—"and Roger knows practically everything about everything." I just didn't have the heart to tell her about all the Rogers on the cohabital landscape—from the inept Rogers whose "handiness" somehow never gets past the talking stage to the truly handy Rogers who nevertheless drag in every night just *after* the hardware store closes. I couldn't bring myself to tell her of all the tales I had heard from disillusioned women which add up to one conclusion: about four out of five men seem to be washouts as home repairers. Whether from busyness, or laziness, or ignorance, or lack of confidence, few men live up to a woman's reasonable expectations of them as repairmen.

Often the repair efforts of even a handy husband take on a distinctly myopic air: *his* carburetor clog gets unclogged but *her* can opener still sticks; *his* electric drill gets oil, but *her* hair dryer continues to shoot sparks; *his* dog gets brushed, while *her* faucet drips on . . . And who can be so naïve to think, when even the *his* jobs aren't all getting done, that the *her* jobs will even get started?

The sad sum of it is, finally, that, for all the cultural dogma that puts a doll carriage under the Christmas tree for a girl when a pair of pliers might be better, the real repairman in the average household is, by default, that girl, now grown, after twenty years of careful protection from anything resembling a tool.

And I have yet to meet the woman who is glad that society "protected" her from all things mechanical and who enjoys knowing that, when a lamp switch fails, her only decision is whether to call the electrician or the trashman. I know of no woman who is proud to own two of everything, just because one of them usually doesn't work.

The fact is that women don't have to be unhandy. They are *not* inherently nonmechanical; they have been educationally deprived by their society and then trained to believe that their aptitude is low. What is most needed is authoritative assurance that "educationally deprived" does not mean "uneducable," and that, in general, the business of making repairs is far easier than most women believe.

* *

If you have the feeling that I have been peeking at your unpublished autobiography; if you resent your growing suspicion that you're going to have to marry a man just to keep your toilet in working order; if you're sick of pleading with your "handyman" to hang your favorite water color—and if you're ready to do something about it, you've come to the right place.

Because this book is for you.

2

How to Get Over That Helpless Feeling

I'll be the first to give sympathetic agreement: that forlorn feeling of utter helplessness sweeping over you in waves as you stand, flickering candle in quivering hand, in front of the glassy-eyed fuse box in your powerless house is perfectly reasonable.

But that perfectly reasonable feeling is your own worst enemy, the barrier between you and the ability to resolve your repair problems, including that ailing fuse box.

The problem is that you're caught and held by your own self-fulfilling prophecy, just as were those residents of that isolated English village who installed their water pipes *outside* their houses so that they would be more accessible for repair if they were to freeze. Your conviction that you're not smart enough or clever enough to be your own maintenance ma'am is your guarantee that you'll never try it.

The fact is that this very understandable feeling is more than self-defeating.

It's wrong.

Do you actually believe that plumbers, electricians, and

refrigerator repairmen are necessarily one bit more intelligent than you are? Do you think that, if they suddenly had to generate a cheese soufflé in a half hour, most of them wouldn't feel just as hopeless as you feel when your hair dryer gasps its last breath thirty minutes before the guests are due? Do you have the impression that your air-conditioner serviceman is automatically a whiz at piecrusts? Or can write absence excuses for his kids in iambic pentameter?

The only difference between a repairman and you is that somebody showed him how. And then gave him a bunch of instruction manuals. Just as you're inclined to say, "Anybody who can read can cook," so he is inclined to say, "Anybody who can read can fix a light switch."

And you're both right.

I speak from experience when I say this, for, since 1970, at Goucher College, in a minimester course called "Nuts and Bolts in Contemporary Society" I have been teaching college women the contents of this book with gratifying results. Women who had never before held a screwdriver were, within a month, repairing toasters, installing wallpaper, replacing auto fenders, and rejuvenating old lamps. People who had never seen a soldering iron had built their own stereo units and television receivers from kits. Students leaving the course returned to relate the pleasure they experienced when they were able to explain to their male friends a thing or two about household plumbing, and many enthusiastic women reported that their self-image had changed and their self-confidence had increased.

In distilling that course into this book, I have retained two particularly important principles: that one learns best by doing, and that one learns first by doing simple things. The chapters that follow will get you into the repair game at the level of baking brownies and stirring up prepared cake mixes.

What you really need in order to overcome the unconfidence barrier that plagues you are the following:

1. Rehearsals for trouble: a carefully programed introduction to some of the gadgets in your house *before*
   they go bad.

2. Detailed, explicit, nontechnical instructions for the
   repair jobs a person without prior experience can
   handle and honest advice specifying which jobs are
   too tough to tackle.

3. Diagnostic help for the crises, with clear instructions
   on how to *find* the trouble as well as instructions
   on how to *cure* the trouble.

4. The assurance that you're not going to be led past
   your ability into a situation where you'll blow yourself
   up or burn the house down.

And that's what the rest of this book is designed to do. It
contains chapters that will assuage your fears and ignorance
about tools (chapter 3), electricity (chapter 6), and plumbing (chapter 9). These all-important chapters are the key to
your successful use of this book and to the removal of your
lack of self-confidence in repair situations. Chapters 6 and 9
contain exercises that will simultaneously train you in some
elementary repair operations and instruct you in the basic
principles of your electrical and plumbing systems. They're
useless unless you actually *do* the exercises—and the time to
do the exercises is *now*—not ten minutes after the lights
blink out.

Chapters 6 (electrical failure), 20 (electrical appliance
failure), and 21 (small appliances) are diagnostic chapters;
turn to them at crisis time for advice on what to do in the
event of equipment failure when you're not sure what has
gone wrong.

Chapters 4 and 22 will help you gain perspective on handling the easiest and toughest of the repair problems, and
the other chapters are loaded with detailed instructions written for the repair neophyte who has been through the basic
exercises in chapters 6 and 10.

But, before you squeeze a pair of pliers, twist the handle of a screwdriver, or even turn too many more of these pages, you are going to have to get over your aversion to hardware stores. . . .

Do you feel as if hardware stores specialize in having every variety of an item except the one you need? Or in having twelve different items all so closely like the thing you need that you don't know which one to buy? Well, take heart—there will come a time when you will wonder how you could once have found it so difficult to locate the right thing. Did you ever notice how long it takes a man to find the cinnamon in a grocery store? And then did you notice the struggle he went through to pick the best brand, best size, and best price? And then did you observe that he picked out stick cinnamon instead of ground cinnamon? That one task undoubtedly kept him occupied long enough for you to finish the rest of the shopping list and find him in time to point out the right box.

I contend that anyone who can enter an unfamiliar grocery store and walk unerringly to the canned peaches (and few women can't) can master a hardware store. All it takes is a few unhurried, browsy trips to get over the desperate feeling that comes when you survey that sea of 3,000 half-filled bins of strange-looking parts, units, assemblies, tools, levers, plugs, tubes, hinges, latches, ladders, zingers, zongers, and general purpose dingbats, convinced that you're going to have to peer into every bin before you find *your* item.

Would you believe that I have had several female students tell me that now they *like* to go to hardware stores just to browse around, read labels, get ideas, and kick wheelbarrow tires? If they could get to the point of enjoying trips to the hardware store, I know that you can get over that nervous aversion that you now have.

So, the next time you need light bulbs (and I'll wager that you need them right now!), don't buy them in the grocery store—they generally charge top prices for light bulbs anyway—go to the hardware store, wander around until you find light bulbs; then, armed with the successful purchase, smile at a salesman or two. You'll be all set up for the next trip, when you may need a little patient help and advice in picking out a few tools.

3

Tools Make Women Handy Too

Since you've read this far, be warned: There is no such thing as doing one or two jobs and stopping. You think it's hard to stop smoking? Once you have saved yourself a $20 bill or two by being handy, you're hooked! Unless you have time galore, don't let your less handy friends and neighbors know that you own this book or that you are on speaking terms with a screwdriver. Which reminds me, that's what this chapter is all about—TOOLS.

If you don't own any tools, you're lucky. You could be saddled with hand-me-down relics that weren't any good when they were new. If you have never bought a tool of any kind, lend an ear; this chapter tells how to do just that. Can you do without tools? Don't kid yourself; instead, wrap your fingers around a good tool and you'll feel strength you didn't suspect you had. Tools are power, and you'll soon be ready to release it and use it.

Good tools are cheap and poor tools are expensive in the long run. In other words, "bargain tools" aren't. And that's telling it exactly like it is. A top-quality tool, properly cared for, will last longer than you will. It'll be around for the next generation and will always be a joy to use. Even better, a quality tool is literally safer than a "cheapie" made of inferior materials poorly designed.

Which explains my grade-A number-one advice: Buy the best quality tools you can afford—or perhaps better—buy the quality tools you can't quite afford.

But what tools are for you? Wondrous and diverse as are the contents of your purse, a tool kit it is not. The jobs at hand call for more than a key or a dime or even a nail file.

So—here we go with a glimpse at what it takes to keep everything running, ringing, hanging, swinging, heating, cooling, opening, closing, pushing, pulling, flushing and filling —at your house.

Drills

Holes, holes, holes! There are holes you make, holes you wish you hadn't made, and holes somebody else made. Drilling holes is one of the most common and useful things you will have to do—and the most frequently botched. But when you know how, it's a breeze.

Take your courage (and charge card) in hand and treat yourself to a ¼″ or a ⅜″ electric drill (the ¼″ and ⅜″ refer to the maximum diameter of "drill bit"—the spiraled shaft that actually cuts the hole—which the drill will hold). It's the greatest invention since the spoon and fork: Light, easy to use, fast, and does the job just right—and not expensive. Besides drilling holes it has all sorts of accessories which you can use with it when the bug really bites you (accessories for buffing, polishing, grinding, sanding, stirring, pumping water, and others).

Don't go off half-cocked and buy some unheard-of clunker because it looks like a bargain. Stick to the well-known brands. The motor name plate should specify a minimum of

2 amp (the amount of electric current, a measure of the drill's power) and the drill speed should be continuously variable; that is, you should be able to control the speed with the pressure of your finger on the trigger. Don't settle for anything less.

At the same time, get a set of drill bits suitable for either wood or metal, ranging in size from 1/16″ to 1/4″, and comparable in quality to your drill. A countersink bit is almost indispensable (see page 151). The salesman will guide you. You are now ready to drill just about anything except an oil well.

HOWEVER, you may still not be convinced that you need an *electric* drill. But that's because you've never had one and

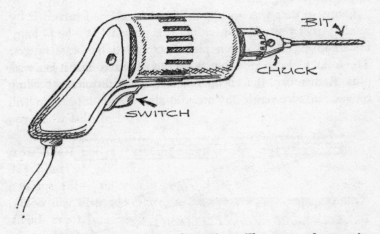

you don't trust me yet. So, if you're still queasy about using a buzzing little machine (you won't be later on), then settle at the moment for a quality hand drill, with the same set of bits we've already talked about above. But remember, an electric drill will do everything a hand drill will and a great deal easier and faster; it doesn't take the strength or elbow grease either. And just think of all those delectable accessories you'll be missing. Here's the clincher: A first-rate hand drill costs about three-fourths as much as a comparable ¼″ electric one.

Folding Rule

Try this: Estimate to the nearest ¹⁄₁₆″ (or 1″ for that matter) the width of your bathroom door. Now verify it with a common ruler. If your estimate was right on the nose, then forget the folding rule.

Okay, so that was an impossible task and you missed it by a mile; treat yourself to a folding rule anyway. It'll be 6′ long, folded in exactly a dozen pieces connected by brass hinges. The small 6″ brass rule that slides out of one end of it is a real plus. Remember, the cheaper the rule the flimsier the brass hinges, and vice versa. Buy accordingly.

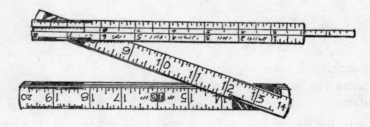

Hammer

Hammers also come in different shapes and sizes and weights. You'll need one, and here's how to pick it: ask for a nail hammer with a curved claw and bell face. This is the usual hammer with which you are familiar. The weight? Try something around 10 to 12 ounces. Pick it up, swing it and see how it feels. Too heavy a hammer is hard to control and too light a hammer produces an exercise in futility.

Did you know that the face of the hammer is ever so slightly angled to fit your swing, greatly increasing your chances of a solid hit on the nail head? What won't they think of next!

Plane

This gem of a tool is a smoother or a shaver of wood—say the edge of a door or a drawer. And the best part: It's designed so that you can't split the wood using it. Not only that, it takes only a little bite at a time, so the situation is always under control.

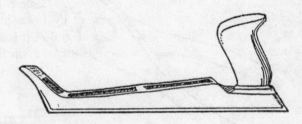

You can't go wrong with either one of the following: a multibladed plane (12"), a block plane (6"), or a jack plane (12"). Perhaps the mutibladed plane is the best as a starter.

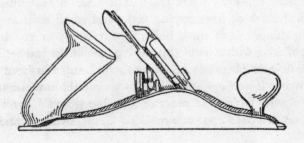

Pliers

Pliers are grippers, and their jaws have teeth to prove it. They come in various shapes and sizes, but two types will let you grab most anything you will need to hold.

Regular (or slip-joint) pliers are the old stand-by, the kind everybody refers to as "a pair of pliers." Real work horses. The jaws can be made to hold in two different positions— one for gripping objects up to about ½" and the other up to about 1". Even good ones are not expensive. If you can find a pair with plastic-covered handles, fine; they're more comfortable to use. The pliers should be about 7" long. By the way, at the base of the jaws is a small wire cutter.

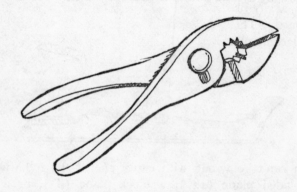

Long-nose or needle-nose pliers look like the front end of a stork and their tapering jaws slip into all sorts of snug places that slip-joint pliers can't. These are a real must for electrical work or for gripping tacks and small nails and for pulling things out of small holes. Be sure the pair you buy is about 7" long with a wire cutter at the base of the jaws.

Needle-nose pliers *can* be used to strip insulation from electrical wires if you are super careful to cut the insulation but *not* the wire. This takes practice and finesse and I don't recommend it. When you start rewiring lamps, making extension

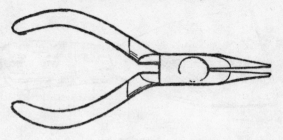

cords, and too many other things to mention, nothing will take the place of a wire stripper, page 20.

If the strength in your hand isn't all you would like it to be (in other words, if your grip is puny)—locking pliers to the rescue. They multiply the strength of your hands, convert it into a vice-like gripping action and, even better, hold it indefinitely. The jaw width is adjustable up to about 1½″ on 9″ locking pliers.

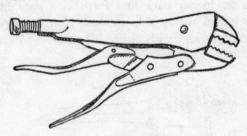

Putty Knife (spackling blade)

It's more like a spatula than a knife, and it's great for spreading stuff on bread and icing cakes, but it can also be used for scraping, puttying, patching holes in walls and ceilings, since, after all, this isn't a cookbook. The blade should be 3″ wide and *flexible*. Clean and dry it after use and it will last from now until then. If your walls have no cracks and you never move a picture and need to patch the hole it leaves behind (or you never ice a cake)—then forget it, you don't need a putty knife.

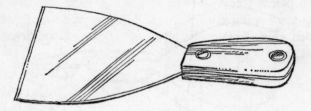

Sander

Face it. You're not going to be able to avoid sanding—smoothing things with sandpaper. The question is: How are those arm muscles? If you would like to firm them up a bit, do your sanding the hard way. Otherwise, be lazy like the rest of us and buy an electric sander, fundamentally an electric vibrator attached to a pad made to hold sandpaper. Choose either a reciprocating or orbital sander. The first moves the sandpaper back and forth in a straight line; the latter provides a rotary side motion. Neither requires great physical strength and with either it's possible to sand in corners.

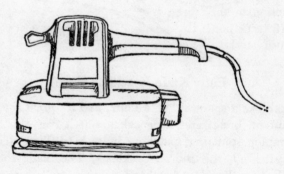

Saw

A crosscut saw is best for general work, but I'll spare you the intricacies of tooth shapes in crosscut, ripsaws, and hacksaws. Ask for a crosscut saw between 20″ and 24″ long, having 8 or 10 points (teeth) per inch. Keep it clean and dry, don't bang the cutting edge against *anything*, and watch out for hidden nails. Remember, this is a saw for cutting wood and wood alone.

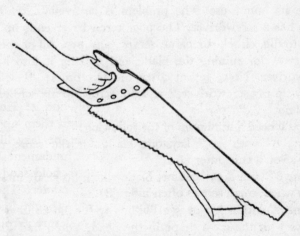

When it comes to the really tough job of cutting metal, the hacksaw's your tool. The tough, relatively short blade is under tension in the frame and its fine teeth (choose a blade with 18 teeth per inch) pointing forward take a real bite on the push stroke. *Never* touch your crosscut wood saw to metal. Leave that for the hacksaw.

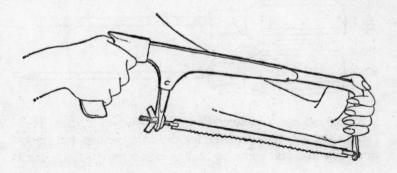

Screwdriver

By all odds the screwdriver is the most used and misused of tools. In spite of its very careful design to perform the single job of turning and driving screws, this frequently turns out to be its minor use. The problem is its availability. *Everybody* has a screwdriver. The poor screwdriver ends up being used to dig, chisel, stir paint, scrape, and pry. All of these are just great for ruining the blade and making it into a lousy screwdriver. Now, repeat after me ten times: "I will not screw up my screwdriver, I will not screw up my screwdriver, I will not . . ."

You'll need a minimum of the following:

One 8" with ⁵⁄₁₆" keystone blade for the more rugged screws you'll encounter (A).

One 8" with a ¼" cabinet blade which fits easily into small holes where small screws often hide (B).

One 8" with a ※1 or ※2 Phillips tip for those rather pretty screws with the cross shape in the head. You'll find Phillips-head screws in all sorts of places, from bathroom fixtures to electrical appliances (C).

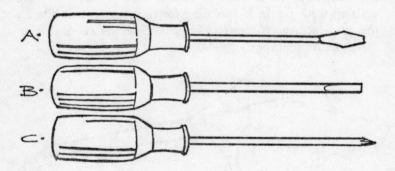

A suggestion: You may find a screwdriver with a ³⁄₁₆" blade absolutely indispensable for those tiny screws you sometimes run into and you may find a large screw that you can't budge without a ⅜″ blade. But you can buy these when the need is clear and present.

Another suggestion: There is such a thing as a screwdriver with a single handle made to accept, and is sold with, blades of assorted sizes (including square and Phillips). "Bargain" screwdrivers of this type are to be shunned like the plague. The metal blades are soft, the handle is weak and the chuck that holds the blades isn't secure in the handle. Buy a good one or stick with quality individual screwdrivers.

One more word. I'll bet you didn't know that the longer and fatter the screwdriver the more powerful turning action you can exert. So, for stubborn screws, use the longest, fattest one that fits the screws.

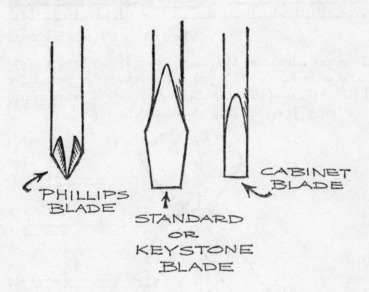

PHILLIPS BLADE

STANDARD OR KEYSTONE BLADE

CABINET BLADE

Square

Maybe you're not square, but what you make will look a whale of a lot better if *it* is. By great good chance there is a uniquely versatile "combination square" which, all in one, is

a square—good for marking off nice crisp right angles—
a level, a measurer of 45° angles, a foot rule, and a straight
edge, among other things. It's difficult even to make a picture
frame without it. By comparison the "common" square really
is that.

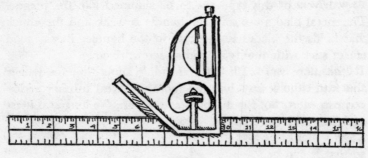

Vise

I am not advocating vice, only a vise. If you have a work-
table or bench to which you can attach one of these super
handy holders of things, you'll be glad you did. Even a small
one (say 3″ jaws) will hold a lot of work for you.

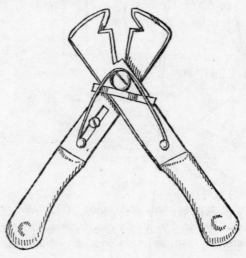

Wire Stripper

This little gadget allows you to cut through the insulation of an electrical wire but *not* through the wire, every time. Its jaws are adjustable to fit the wire you are stripping and worth its weight in temper lost trying to strip wires any other way.

Wood Chisel

It looks like a super wide screwdriver with a beveled end, and that end should be as sharp as a knife (which it is). Chisels come in all sorts of sizes but you will find one with $\frac{1}{4}''$ blade and one with a $\frac{3}{4}''$ blade just right. The blade should be 4" to 5" long; be sure the handle has a metal cap on the top so that it can be tapped with a hammer. Buy a really cheap one and you chisel yourself.

Wrench

Wrenches, like pliers, are grippers, but with a difference. Wrenches are made to fit snugly to a regularly shaped object—like a nut on a bolt; for each size nut there's a certain size wrench. There are also adjustable wrenches; set them to fit something and they hold on tighter than pliers usually can.

Of the wide variety of wrench types available, you'll find the most generally useful are: two adjustable ("crescent") wrenches, one 6" long and the other 10" long. Between them they can handle fittings up to $1\frac{1}{8}''$ and that's just about anything you will meet. The jaw faces are smooth and a properly fitted adjustable wrench will not scar or in any way damage a fitting. On the other hand, the jaws of pliers have teeth and should never be used on regularly shaped (square, hexagonal or octagonal) fittings. Your two adjustable wrenches will take the place of a multitude of sizes of "fixed" wrenches.

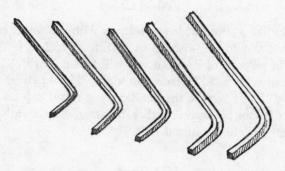

Hexagonal ("hex") or Allen wrenches are another breed of cat: They're straight rods of hexagonal steel bent in a right angle at one end. Have you ever seen a screw with a six-sided hole in its head? If you ever have to loosen (or tighten) one of these, *nothing* but a "hex" wrench will do. They can be bought separately or in sets.

A pipe wrench is an adjustable one with jaws full of teeth. Just as the name says, *use it only on pipes.* In fact, only on *iron* pipes. It has terrific gripping action and allows you to exert great torque or turning action, but leaves tooth marks wherever it's been.

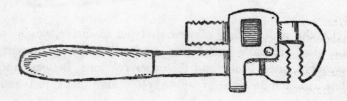

CARE AND FEEDING OF TOOLS

Maintenance Do's

1. *Do* save and file any instruction sheets.
2. *Do* keep tools clean and dry.
3. *Do* inspect electrical cords, before and after each use, for cuts, abrasions, or breaks in insulation—and repair them if necessary.
4. *Do* lubricate regularly if there are moving parts, but *don't* soak your tools in oil (follow that instruction sheet).

Safety Don'ts

1. *Don't* wear clothes with long loose sleeves, jewelry or anything that can get caught in the moving parts of a tool.
2. *Don't* let long hair fall forward into a moving tool; tie it back, wrap it, put it up—even cut it—but keep it out of the way.

Right! I haven't said a word about how to use all these goodies. But relax, that's coming up in the chapters ahead.

TOOL LIST

Here's a list of basic tools. Show it to the people at the hardware store. (Find a real hardware store, if you can, not just a housewares store.) Some of the terms below are as yet unexplained, but you'll be introduced to them further along in the book.

E=Electrical; P=Plumbing; G=General
*Minimum Set for Electrical and Plumbing Repairs

Chisel (G)

1 wood chisel, ¼" blade,
5" long, with metal cap

1 wood chisel, ¾" blade,
5" long, with metal cap

Drain Auger (P)

*1 drain auger, 10' (also
called a snake)

Drill, Electric (G)

1 ¼" electric drill,
continuously variable
speed

Drill, Hand (G)

1 hand drill

Drill Bits (G)

1 set drill bits for wood and
metal, ¹⁄₁₆" to ¼"
1 countersink bit

1 masonry bit (size
determined by anchor size
used)

Drill, Star (G)

1 star drill (size determined
by anchor size used)

File (G)

1 wood file, half-round, 10"

Hammer, Nail (G)

1 nail hammer, 13 oz.

Light, Trouble (G)

1 trouble light with 15' cord
(good for working in dark
places)

Nail Set (G)

1 nail set, 1/16" tip

Plane (G)

1 multiblade plane, 10"   or 1 jack plane, 12"

Pliers (E, G)

1 regular, 6"   1 locking type, 6" to 8"
*1 needlenose, with wire
cutter, 4" to 6"

Plunger (P)

*1 plunger (force cup)   1 toilet plunger (Toilaflex)

Putty Knife (Spackling blade) (G)

1 putty knife, 3" blade,
flexible

Rule

1 folding rule, 6′

Sander, Electrical (G)

1 orbital electrical sander

Sandpaper (G)

1 assortment

Saw (G)

1 crosscut saw, 8 pts. or 11 pts.   1 hacksaw

Screwdriver (E, P, G)

*1 cabinet blade screwdriver, 8″, ¼″ tip

*1 standard blade screwdriver, 8″, 5⁄16″ tip

*1 Phillips, ⚏P–2

Square (G)

1 combination square

Tape, Electrical (E)

*1 roll ½″ black plastic electrical tape

Wire Cutter (E)

*1 diagonal wire cutter, 4″ to 6″

Wire Stripper (E)

* 1 wire stripper, 6"

Wrench, Adjustable (E, P, G)

*1 adjustable wrench, 10"   *1 adjustable wrench, 6"

Wrench, Crescent (G)

1 crescent wrench, 10"

4

Fifty Per Cent of Your Repair Problems Aren't

The local radio repair shop flatly refused to touch it, and the proprietor tried instead to interest the elderly couple in a new stereo unit, but Social Security benefits don't buy stereo rigs, and besides, their good old 1949 Capehart radio-phonograph was too much a member of the family to be discarded. I myself had worked on it for them three or four times, but finally the record changer had simply stopped dead. Parts were unavailable, and we were about to play taps over this fine-sounding unit when suddenly an idea struck me.

That unit works splendidly today, and the final repair required not a single tool and cost perhaps $.06.

* *

My wife had complained about it for nearly five years, and I can't blame her—the window on her side of the bed was so difficult to open that she was bending the crowbar that I had thoughtfully painted green to match the curtains. Finally one warm night, when she quietly announced that there would be a new window, air conditioning, or separate bedrooms, I decided that the time was ripe for a little window work. I'm actually embarrassed to tell you that I cured that five-year-old problem without tools in about two and a half minutes for about a dime.

* *

Even before reaching my locked front door, I would routinely feel anger welling up on the inside of me—only two years earlier I had bought the best lock in the hardware store, and within a year the lock had developed a severe bulldog complex—once the key had been turned, it took the patience of Job and the fine touch of Houdini to get it back out.

Today the lock operates better than new as a result of a "repair" job that required less than a minute.

* *

My secret weapon in each of these cases was exactly the same thing: an aerosol spray can of silicone lubricant. The offending keyhole got a couple of short bursts before I inserted the key; the window got sprayed wherever two surfaces had to slide; the phonograph turntable simply got doused from underneath wherever any moving part contacted another moving part. This amazing stuff is worth its weight in Pingpong balls, and I'm sure I haven't discovered all of its uses yet.

Do you have a refrigerator door that squeaks or a kitchen cabinet door that opens stiffly? Spray the hinges. Do you have a screen door that latches reluctantly or whose latch sticks in the open position instead of springing spontaneously back to the latch position? A good snort of silicone lubricant in every likely opening of that latch may cure it. How about a manual typewriter with a sticking key? Guess at where the undue friction is, point the spray, and save yourself a $30 typewriter overhaul. Maybe your car door sticks in the open position (give the hinges a squirt), or your hood latch requires three slams before it's closed (give it to all parts of that offending latch). Does your silverware drawer grate just a little, and do your jalousies work more stiffly than they did last year? Does the flap on your forced-air register stick in a certain fixed position, or does the motor in your hair dryer have an irritating squeak? Silicone spray lubricant is the pressurized genie that can bottle up all of these problems. The stuff works miracles on reluctant breadbox covers, squeaky bar stools, and arthritic folding chairs. Almost anything that slides (Teflon is the chief exception) slides better with a silicone film to help it—even the zipper on your dress (although, since it may indelibly spot the fabric, it is best to spray a little lubricant on your finger and run the finger over the teeth of the zipper).

As a class of compounds, silicones are not only slippery, they're chemically unreactive, commonly stable at temperatures as high as 400° F and very nonvolatile; they're completely hydrophobic (like paraffin, refusing to let water wet it), and have an extremely low surface energy (almost all surfaces like to be covered by a film of silicone). This means that, in addition to lubricating, a can of silicone spray will waterproof your golf shoes, rustproof your tools and auto chrome, stop snow from sticking to your snow shovel, and, if you spray it onto your oven surfaces after its next cleaning, will make the oven easier to clean the following time.

I've heard of kindergarten teachers who spray the inside of every pair of galoshes and rubbers that walks into their classrooms to make them easy to reinstall at three o'clock, campers who have used it as an emergency leak stopper in their tent (although it did leave a permanent stain), drivers who spray the rubber gaskets of their car doors and trunk to keep them from freezing shut, homeowners who spray the rubber gaskets and interior surfaces of their non-frost-free freezers to facilitate ice removal, skiers who spray their ski bindings to protect them from freezing.

Buy yourself a can of this instant wizard, and I suspect

that, before the can is empty, you will have cured dozens of household problems and devised a novel application of your own.

BUT IT DOESN'T DO QUITE EVERYTHING!

There are just a few things this stuff doesn't manage to do—balance the books, for example, or take out the garbage. There are even a few lubrication jobs it can't handle, and I feel compelled to tell you about them. They involve electric motors.

For our purposes right now, electric motors can be divided into three classes: the tiny, rather cheaply built motors that run many phonographs, electric clocks, and very small fans such as those portable space heaters belong to the first class. If these squeak, growl, or run erratically, a shot of silicone spray at the point where the shaft enters the motor case may be the cure. And a few miscellaneous shots in other likely looking openings won't hurt, and may even help.

The second class consists of motors with factory sealed bearings which should never need lubrication; these will usually be labeled "Do not oil" or "Sealed bearings." The third class contains motors which require oil in specific locations. The manufacturers, for reasons beyond me, generally assume that all owners will know what to do in the absence of any instructions whatever. They assume that, if you have a large window fan, an attic fan, a sump pump, or a forced-air heating system, you will notice the complete absence of advice on the motors involved and conclude that you must do the following:

1. Have on hand a can of household oil.
2. Locate one hole on each end of the motor that looks like it leads to the rotating shaft. The hole is usually about the diameter of the lead in a wood pencil; sometimes it's plugged with a bright red plug; occasionally it is covered by a little cap held shut by a spring.

3. Get about two drops of oil into each hole about once a year.

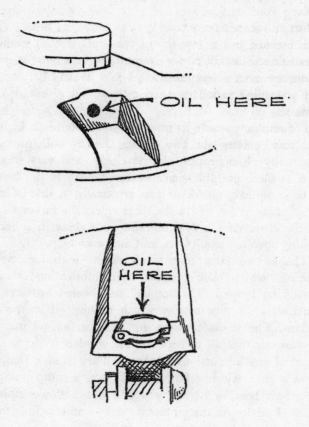

Not long ago I noticed that the warm-air ducts in my home were emitting, in addition to hot air, a new sound. It sounded a little like a squeak with laryngitis, best described as a "dry" sound. After turning the furnace off, I located the air blower and motor in the back of the furnace, found two dry oil holes, contributed a few drops of oil, and restarted the furnace. Within sixty seconds the noise subsided.

I breathed a sigh of relief, knowing that I had just prevented a $65 expenditure a month later.

Keep your ears peeled for such changes in the sound of motors; do something about it as soon as you hear a change —an increase in noise (but don't be confused by rattles and vibrations) or a "dry" sound—and you will be saving many headaches and dollars in the long run.

If you think you have a motor in need of oil and can't locate the oil holes, you have what I consider a very reasonable question to ask a friend who is handy. She'll undoubtedly be flattered that you asked her.

5

How Not to Get a Charge Out of Your Electrical System

Remember how he strode into your house last spring? Complete with low-slung gunbelt full of screwdrivers and fancier tools, he swaggered like a displaced extra from a grade-B Western across your living room rug with the dramatic words, "OK, lady, where's your fuse box?" Twenty minutes later your light switch was working again, your best carpet had a case of dirty footprints, and your hand held a bill for the better part of your income for the day: You needed that electrician and he knew it—and suddenly you knew that he knew!

There are three important things about the expensive service he performed for you: first, the task he performed was very simple—much simpler than solving a quadratic equation or playing the piano. Second, he was not at any time in the slightest danger of getting electrocuted (remember how he turned off the house current and made your electric clock lose fifteen valuable minutes instead?). Third, the procedure he followed was something that he learned, and something that you'll learn too; by the end of chapter 8 you'll be replacing your own light switches (among other things) and saving a dozen dollars every time you do.

I don't care if you barely know how to change a light bulb; I don't care if your mother was scared by a short circuit a month before you were born; I don't even care if you are as thoroughly inexperienced as a friend of mine who didn't know that three-way lamps required three-way bulbs for the full effect. If you take an hour or two to perform the simple learning procedures that appear on the following pages, you will be able to make 90% of your own electrical repairs by following the instructions outlined in chapter 7.

Now, here is the most important sentence on this page: In order to make all the repairs described in chapter 7, the "dry run" exercises that follow are an absolute must! Follow the procedures carefully and you can be assured of safety and success; if you try tackling chapters 6 and 7 without the experience gained from these exercises, you are in for a real shock.

I had better be honest at this point, however: The next few pages, no matter how assiduously practiced, do not provide magic carpet conveyance into the electricians' union, Local 698. These gentlemen, complete with training and experience, are still very nice to have for the other 10% of the electrical problems. We'll talk about the jobs you *shouldn't* tackle (if you're a novice) at the end of chapter 21.

Now, on to the exercises, with just a little learning about the nature of electricity sandwiched between each one.

Exercise 1: Stop Ignoring the Inner Being of Your Light Bulbs

Light bulbs are like dandelions—if they weren't so common we would write poems about their beauty and sing songs about their worth. Instead, we complain about their cost and grumble when they die.

Pick up an ordinary "one-speed" light bulb (with just

one wattage stamped on it) and marvel for a minute at the intricacy of this device for which you have paid less than the cost of a chocolate milk shake. To make this bulb, someone has created a seamless glass globe, frosted it evenly, fused it flawlessly to a glass post through which two fine wires pass, and delicately welded between the tip of these two wires, at the center of the frosted globe, a miniscule coil of tungsten wire whose diameter is less than 0.001 inch. Then somebody sealed the globe, pumped all the air out of it, and fastened to it two pieces of metal with a black insulator between them. Someone then tested, packed, shipped, and marketed these amazing devices for roughly the price of a good shoeshine— and made a profit to boot! The automobile may be a monument to spectacular American ingenuity, but the light bulb is the simplest symbol of quiet American efficiency.

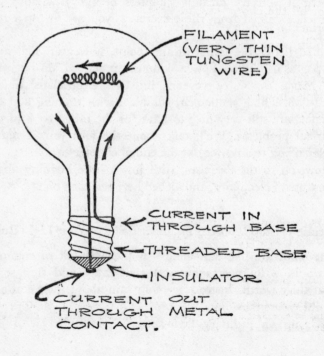

FILAMENT
(VERY THIN
TUNGSTEN
WIRE)

CURRENT IN
THROUGH BASE

THREADED BASE

INSULATOR

CURRENT OUT
THROUGH METAL
CONTACT.

Rotate the bulb until you find what looks like a flaw in the threaded metal portion at the edge where it joins the glass. This is actually a tiny, welded junction through which current flows from the threaded portion of the base of the bulb into one of the wires feeding into the center of the bulb. From there the current flows through the tungsten filament (which, because it has moderately high resistance to the flow of the current being forced through it, gets hot and glows appropriately), then passes back down the other "feed" wire, which has been thoughtfully attached to the piece of metal at the very center of the base. The black insulating material (a type of porcelain) has such extremely high resistance that it's impossible for current to flow from the threaded metal to the center metal disc without taking the long route through the filament.

For all the clever engineering that a light bulb represents, its principle is delightfully simple: electric current flows into the bulb at one point (the threaded socket), around a loop (which includes the filament), and back out at another point (the center of the base).[1] A thorough understanding of this principle is practically all you need to understand your household wiring well enough to make most repairs.

Now you're ready to see how this principle operates in the next exercise:

Exercise 2: Gaze Freely into the Socket of Your Favorite Table Lamp!

Walk casually over to the nearest table lamp that uses a standard screw-type "one-speed" bulb and, grasping the body of its wall plug, disconnect it from the socket of the wall

---

[1] Purists may be worrying at this point about which way the current really flows. Actually, it flows first one way for $\frac{1}{120}$th of a second, then the other way for $\frac{1}{120}$th of a second before reversing again, thus making 60 complete cycles per second; whence the name "60 cycle AC," or "60 cycle alternating current."

outlet. Now, armed with the knowledge that 99.9% of all lamps have removable shades (the exceptions are contemporary-style gooseneck lamps with conical shades and switches at the center of the shades), study your lamp and decide what must be done to remove its shade. I'll bet you ten to one that you have already noticed that the fancy crown at the top center of the shade is really a threaded nut that can be unscrewed (by turning it counterclockwise, just as you would loosen the cap on a catsup bottle) to release the shade. If that nut doesn't unscrew quite readily for you, give the whole shade a counterclockwise turn (about an eighth of a turn should do) and try it again.

After you unscrew the bulb, you'll notice that the socket is equipped with a metal conductor, positioned to touch the center of the bulb socket. You have probably noticed that little piece of metal before—but I'll wager that you never before noticed that on the outside of the socket is stamped the word PRESS. See it? It's right next to the switch.

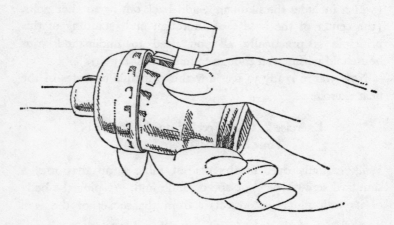

Well, what are you waiting for? Grasp the neck of that lamp and squeeze that socket for all it's worth, with your thumb covering the word PRESS and pushing both in and up.

Voilà! Suddenly the socket has fallen apart in your hands, and you are able to see that the socket consists of four simple parts, as pictured below.

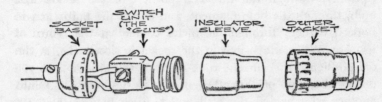

After removing the barrel and the insulator, take a good look at the socket and the two wires that feed it. You can now see the salient parts of a much larger electrical loop which includes the light bulb as a small but important part. Here we go:

The current flows out of a wire behind the wall outlet into one of the prongs of the plug, then through *one* of the insulated copper wires (you *did* notice that the lamp cord

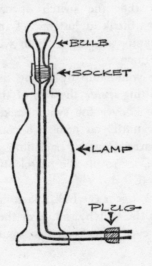

really contains not one but a pair of wires which are insulated from each other, didn't you?), enters the base of the lamp, and flows right up through the screw on the socket assembly, through the threaded portion of the socket and bulb, through the bulb filament, and out of the bulb (as you noticed earlier) through the metal contact at the center of its base. When the switch in the socket is closed (i.e. in the ON position), the current runs through the switch, into the other wire, out of the other prong of the plug, and into another wire behind the wall outlet. Even behind the wall, the loop is extended, such that one could trace an electrical loop all the way from the power station, through your light bulb, and back again to the power plant.

Just a single break in this loop anywhere along the line stops the flow of electrons just as a clamp on a hose stops the flow of all water. And this is precisely the function of the switch, which is nothing more that two pieces of metal which touch in the ON position and separate when one turns the switch off. Notice that the switch opens and closes the circuit by creating a break in just one of the two wires that feed the bulb. Creating a break in both wires is redundant, and isn't ordinarily done.

Now, reassemble your lamp by sliding the barrel and the corrugated edges fitting *inside* the rim of the base. Push the insulting sheath back over the switch-socket unit, with the barrel down firmly until you hear two comforting clicks as each side of the barrel snuggles back into place. Just to be sure that it's secure, try to lift the barrel off the base; if you fail, you've succeeded.

Back into the socket goes the bulb; back into the wall outlet goes the plug. Flick the switch, and savor the warm glow of a lamp that works, even after you disassembled part of the switch!

Exercise 3: Find Your Faithful Fuse Box

There is one more very important switch that's a part of every single electrical loop (or circuit) in your house—it's a switch that turns the current off every time too much current flows. This happens either when too many appliances are simultaneously in use in one part of the house or when the current gets a chance to pass directly from the "inbound" wire to the "outbound" wire without doing some work (such as lighting the filament of a bulb or running a motor) in between, to which everyone applies the euphemism "short circuit." This switch, called a fuse, stands between you and the destruction of your house by a fire resulting from overheating or sparking of wires. The extra heat causes a wire in the fuse to melt, creating a break in the circuit that remains broken until the fuse is replaced.

If you live in a house with a basement, you'll find your fuse box down there, almost directly below the point at which the main power line feeds into your house from the nearest power pole.

If you live in a basementless house or an apartment, your fuse box could be almost anywhere hidden behind a mysterious-looking little door. Although they're usually in the utility room or kitchen, I've seen them in closets, in kitchens, hidden behind the draperies in bedrooms, even in the center of a dining room wall, where the owner had to hide it with a picture!

If you have never found your fuse box, do it right now. Yank open its cover, and compare your panel with the illustrations below. If your panel looks like figure (A) it's because your house is among the majority of homes wired for 115 volts; a panel like figure (B) is typical of homes equipped with 230 volts as well, supplying electric ranges, ovens, hot

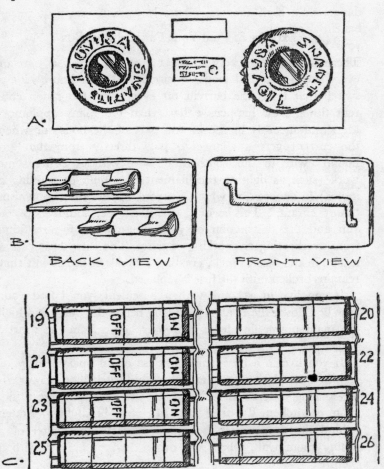

water heater, and dryer. If your panel looks like figure (C),
you are viewing a bit of evidence of a well-built home—
costing somewhat more than a fuse box, your circuit-breaker
panel performs the same function as fuses simply by automatically flipping a resettable switch under conditions of

dangerously high current flow. Of course, you will never benefit from the character-building experience of blowing your last fuse late Saturday evening, but you can find substitutes for this, I'm sure.

Exercise 4: Remove a Fuse or Two

On the door of the fuse box should be a chart indicating precisely which circuits are affected by each circuit breaker or fuse. If the chart has not been completed, the electrician who wired your house was negligent (but normal). If you take a few minutes to fill in the chart now, you may save time and prevent confusion later.

The process is simple. Disconnect one fuse at a time (or flip one circuit-breaker switch off), then send your kids flying through the house looking for lights and appliances that don't work. A desk lamp or hand mixer, carried to the various wall sockets, will identify the turned-off wall sockets quite efficiently.

The round glass-paneled fuses are easily removed: The circuit-breaker switches are easily switched to OFF; but a word is in order about the fuses that supply power to the high-voltage fixtures[2]: Pull firmly on the handgrip that presents itself to you, exposing the fuses shown in the figure below. These fuses, unlike the glass-paneled fuses (which blacken when blown), give no visual evidence of blowing and must be replaced whenever there is a doubt. When you replace this high-voltage fuse holder, *be sure to replace it without inverting it*. If you invert the holder, it will probably remain in a disconnected configuration. Because my own fuse holders are completely unmarked, I have marked mine with a small piece of adhesive tape at the top.

[2] All electric ranges, built-in electric ovens, electric water heaters, and electric dryers; some air conditioners, oil burners, and room heating units.

You'll notice that one fuse is different and/or larger than all the rest of the fuses; this fuse almost never fails and often doubles as the main power switch (turn power off by pulling it out). If, however, after a power loss due to an

electrical storm, your neighbors regain power and you alone sit in blackness, don't become paranoid—replace your main fuse.

Exercise 5: Discover That Your Light Switch Has Connections

Most houses are equipped with two types of light switches. The simpler of the two types, called a single pole (or two-way) switch, is the type used where a single switch operates one or more fixtures. The second, called three-way, is employed wherever two switches operate the same fixture, such as one finds in a hall or on a stairway.

The first is used in a delightfully simple circuit, diagramed below;

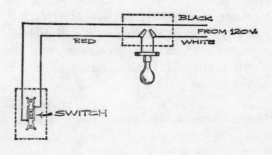

the second is part of a masterpiece of simple ingenuity whose operation is explained in the diagrams below. You'll notice

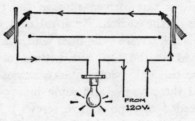

CIRCUIT IS COMPLETE WHEN BOTH SWITCHES ARE DOWN:

FROM 120V.

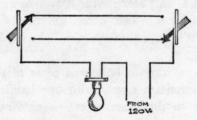

BUT CIRCUIT IS BROKEN WHEN EITHER SWITCH IS CHANGED:

FROM 120V.

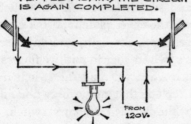

AND, IF EITHER SWITCH IS FLIPPED AGAIN, THE CIRCUIT IS AGAIN COMPLETED.

FROM 120V.

that three-way switches require three electrical connections, while two-way need only two.[3]

[3] If you have a light that is operated by three or more switches, both the circuitry and the switches are more complicated.

Pick a single pole light switch and turn it on; then go to the fuse box and unscrew the fuse which affects that light. Return to the light switch and flick it off and on to verify that it is no longer operative.

Using a medium screwdriver, remove the two screws in the cover plate of the switch. Removal of the cover plate will reveal two more screws—the ones which hold the switch in place—located at the top and bottom of the opening which you have exposed. (Sometimes a recent wallpapering job has covered these screws and some judicious excising of wallpaper is needed to expose these screws.) Remove these two screws, then grasp the switch assembly and pull out from the wall two or three inches. If it resists, don't give up—it *will* come, and along with it will come two stiff insulated copper wires which carry the power through the switch (when it's on), through the light, and around the loop.

Now, there's nothing to be scared of in this switch; grab one of the two contact screws with one hand and touch a tentative finger to the other screw—See? Nothing. If you had not removed the fuse, there would be a you-shaped engraving on the ceiling, but—fuse out, danger gone.

Push wires and switch back into the switch box; replace the switch screws, the cover plate, and the cover plate screws. Replace the fuse, check the light, and enjoy seeing one more thing which has survived your inquisitive fingers!

Did you notice when you had the switch out, that, if you had wanted to replace that noisy, brown-handled thing with a new, silent, white-handled mercury switch, it would have been eminently simple? Release the wires from beneath the screws of the old switch; tighten them beneath the only two available screws on the new switch (the order doesn't even matter) and push the new switch into place—that's $15 you have saved already.

You're ready now to tackle most of your electrical problems, make your own repairs, and save real dollars. The next three chapters are filled with detailed instructions and important tips for maintaining the electrical system of your home.

6

Electrical Diagnosis

WHAT'S WRONG?

Just beyond your closed window, a blanket of fresh snow is building rapidly enough to give assurance that you can sleep late tomorrow. Oak logs are snapping brightly in the fireplace. The doors are all secure; the phone is off the hook; your coffee maker and popcorn popper are about to deliver the evening's treat; your stereo is sounding better than ever as you snuggle into your favorite chair. Precisely as you open your book, the stereo fades, your reading light blinks off, the coffee maker stops perking, and reality overwhelms you. In the crisis of the moment, what do you do?

For one thing, sit back and relax for a minute. Contemplate the situation slowly enough to recognize that your first problem has nothing to do with how to fix it—but has everything to do with "What's wrong, and what needs to be fixed?" Your first need is not for a repairman, but for a diagnostician.

In the rest of this chapter, I'll tell you exactly how to diagnose general electrical troubles in the house; then chapter 7 will give detailed instructions for making the repairs and effecting the cures.

The general principle underlying the intelligent diagnosis of electrical problems is delightfully simple:

A properly functioning electrical circuit necessarily involves a complete loop for the current to travel, including a section in which the electricity either does work (such as running a motor) or produces heat or light. Electrical troubles are always the result of either a break somewhere in the loop (called "an open circuit") or the accidental creation of a new loop in which the current comes and goes without doing any work or lighting any lights (a "short circuit"). If you understand this principle, you're already halfway to your AED[1] degree. Now you're ready for the other half:

All Lights and Electric Appliances in House Fail

Check neighboring houses. If any others are powerless, get out your candles, relax, and at your leisure, call[2] the power company for an estimate of the length of your candlelight period. Turn off the burners on your electric range in case power is restored when you are out of the kitchen.

If your house alone is powerless (and this is very unusual), then either your power line has been severed or your main house fuse has blown. Either of these possibilities indicates a problem which should be left to the professionals; contact the power company for assistance. The one exception to this rule is the case in which your power loss results from an overenthusiastic visit from a lightning bolt, in which case it is safe to replace the main fuse.

A Circuit Fuse Blows or Circuit Breaker Trips

You have either created a short circuit or have overloaded the circuit with too many appliances.

[1] Amateur Electrical Diagnostician.
[2] Sure, you can call—your phone uses a separate power supply.

Overloading a circuit is surprisingly easy to do, and this is the first possibility to consider. Air conditioners and all heat-producing appliances take large amounts of energy, and all it takes to blow a 15-amp fuse is about 1725 watts, so a toaster (1150 watts) and an electric griddle (1500 watts) on the same line would be guaranteed to polish off any 15-amp fuse. Even a 20-amp fuse (which handles a maximum of 2300 watts) would yield to this combination. This leads some foolhardy people to replace their fuses with 30-amp fuses (which carry 3450 watts), thereby inviting the possibility of fire from overheated house wiring instead. In general:

1. Thirty amp fuses don't belong in 115-volt circuits.
2. A burned fuse should be replaced with a fuse whose ampere rating matches its predecessor's.

If you find that you are frequently blowing fuses due to appliance overloading, an electrician can save you money in the long run by putting heavily used outlets onto new circuits with separate fuses.

A short circuit isn't hard to find, although you may burn out another fuse or two while making your diagnosis. Just go through the check list below:

1. Undo the last thing you did before blowing the fuse.
2. Locate in the fuse box the fuse whose glass face reveals a blackened interior. Replace it with a new fuse of equal amperage rating. You will find either that the lights have been restored or that you have simply sacrificed another fuse and the lights are still out.

   If lights are *not* restored:

   (a) Unplug everything in sight and turn off every fixture that depends on the affected fuse. Examine each wall outlet for foreign objects (e.g. a bobby pin) or for a smudge of smoke. If you find a bobby pin, the cure is obvious; if you find evidence of smoke or heat at one of the sockets, the trouble could be either in the outlet or in the plug that you removed. You'll know which it is after you take the next step.

(b) Install a new fuse. If it blows with nothing going, it's the wall socket. Follow instructions on page 70 to replace it. If you don't see a suspicious wall socket, and the new fuse blew, it's time to call an electrician.

(c) If you got through step (b) with a healthy fuse, start plugging things in and turning lights on. You'll finally come to the culprit. The fuse will blow once more, and you're ready to move to (d) below.

If lights are restored:
You know the culprit and wonder only about what part of the culprit caused its culpritness.

(d) Make sure the defective unit is unplugged.

(e) Sniff for the smell of burned insulation; feel for a warm spot (caused by arcing—electricity jumping from wire to wire). The hot spot or smelly spot is it.

(f) If your act that blew the fuse was to employ a switch on an appliance, suspect the switch, or a more serious defect within the unit. Unfortunately, it's usually the latter.

(g) If your fuse-blowing act was to insert a plug into an outlet, suspect the plug, the appliance wire, and the switch. It's wise (and fairly cheap) to replace all three if the problem isn't obvious. See chapter 7.

Once in a blue moon I find that I can go through the entire procedure above, find nothing wrong, plug everything back in, get everything working, and the system acts as if it scared itself into behaving.

There are three possibilities:
1. The fuse itself was defective, or it had been weakened by a near overload on a previous occasion.

2. A speck of metal or stray strand of wire which caused the short circuit got so hot that it melted into a harmless blob, never to be noticed again.

3. One of the lamp or appliance wires on the circuit causes a short circuit only when it's in a certain position. To check for this vigorously wiggle every electrical cord at the plug end and the appliance end to see if you can create a short circuit. If you can make it misbehave, you'll want to follow the procedure on page 72.

The Electric Range or Electric Oven Won't Work

Check your automatic timer. Ninety-nine times out of a hundred some eager-beaver house guest, helping you cook, has turned the clock controlled switch to the automatic position, all ready to turn your oven on full blast at 3:30 A.M.

Check the appropriate multibreaker or fuses. Your fuse unit will either use two 30-amp glass fuses or two 30-amp cardboard-covered cylinders with metal ends, which give no indication of their condition. They're called bayonet-type fuses, and my experience is that they occasionally peter out for no obvious reason. Your best bet, if your cold-hearted oven or range has bayonet fuses, is simply to assume they're bad and replace them with fuses of equal amperage.

If the unit is still chilly, the problem becomes a job for an electrician. These units, along with your electric water heater and electric clothes dryer, are 230-volt devices and are quite unforgiving of even small mistakes.

A Fuse Blows When Your Air Conditioner Turns On

Electric motors, unlike heaters, are quite miserly with electricity—with one exception: during the split second that it takes to get them to full speed, they may soak up almost ten times their rated currents. (This is the reason for the very brief light-dimming action of your sump pump or your air conditioner when they turn on.) This means that under some conditions your fuse will interpret this brief burst of current needed to start a motor as a short circuit and will promptly blow itself out. The cure to this problem is to replace your standard fuses with slow-blow fuses of the same rating. They cost a little more, but are well worth the difference. They are designed to absorb current surges of reasonable size for about a quarter of a second or less, but will protect you against continuous overloads and short circuits with the same faithful fervor of the standard fuse. Incidentally, before you sally forth for fuses, read pages 41–44.

You Insert a Plug into an Outlet and Get an Unscheduled Fourth of July at the Plug

Relax. Catch your breath. Steady your nerves.

Observe that, in your paroxysm of fright, you (probably) have already yanked the plug back out of the socket. If not, it doesn't matter. Do the following:

1. Go to the fuse box and remove the fuse that protects the affected outlet. (Notice whether it has blown—your chances are about one in five that it's still good.
2. Return to the outlet and remove the offending plug. Replace the fuse.
3. The trouble almost always lies in the plug rather than the outlet. Replace the old plug with a new one, following the procedure outlined on page 72.
4. Check the outlet by plugging into it a lamp or appliance which you know to be functioning. It is quite unlikely that you'll see another fireworks dis-

play; you're more likely to find that outlet is now dead because the contacts have been melted away. If so, replace the outlet, following the procedure on page 70.

Three-Way Bulb Won't Light
on All Three Brightness Settings

There's nothing magic about a three-way bulb—it's simply a dual filament bulb with a slightly different base from a standard bulb.

Look into the socket of a three-way lamp and you'll see an extra finger, located off center, reaching straight up to make contact with the metal ring at the base of a three-way bulb.

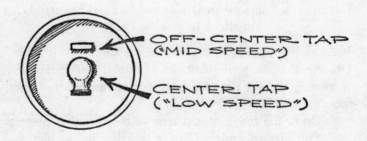

"Low intensity" on a 50–200–250-watt bulb runs current in at the threaded portion of the base, through the 50-watt filament, and out at the metal ring—but only if the ring is making good contact with that extra finger in the socket.

"Mid intensity" uses the 200-watt filament, which is wired between the threaded portion of the base and the center metal tip on the base.

"High intensity" simply uses both filaments together. That's why the high-intensity wattage is always the sum of the other two. That's also why, when one filament burns out, you're left, not with a two-way bulb, but with an ordinary one-way bulb—there's only one filament remaining.

But many perfectly fine three-way bulbs end up in the trash before they deserve to, just because of a poor contact in the socket. Ninety per cent of three-way bulb problems are curable by the first item on the list of procedures below.

1. Tighten the bulb into the lamp socket. Nothing changed? Tighten the bulb a little more—occasionally it is difficult to get the off-center finger in the socket to make contact with the metal ring on the bulb.

2. Replace the bulb. *But don't throw that old bulb away!* If the low wattage filament is burned out and the high wattage filament is still whole, you have a perfectly good standard light bulb whose wattage corresponds to the mid-speed value on the bulb. If the other filament is the one that's burned out— into the trash it goes. Just check it in any standard socket.

3. If the new bulb is no better, *unplug the lamp* for some minor surgery. Look into the socket and notice that the center finger is grayish instead of bronze. It didn't start off that way, and became discolored only as many hours of high temperatures created an oxide layer which worsened the contact with the bulb, thereby creating higher temperatures, thereby creating more oxide, thereby . . . With a small screwdriver, ice pick or sharp knife scratch around on that center tap until you see more brass (or silver) than gray. Then, quite gingerly, lift the center tap from its squashed position until it can act with just a little resilience again. (If this gentle lifting does nothing more than snap off the center contact, don't despair: The socket should have been replaced in the first place. Proceed to step 4.

4. If you still don't have three brightness levels, the

time is at hand for replacement of the socket-switch unit, and you are ready to take advantage of chapter 7, page 75.

Some Bulbs Are So Hard to Screw In and Out That You Barely Get the Bulb to Make Contact, and Your Light Has "the Flickers"

There are three places where corrosion—and the resultant hard-to-screw light bulb—is a chronic problem: outdoor fixtures, recessed ceiling fixtures, and contemporary decor lamps with conical metal shades for spotlight effects. The reason for the first is usually moisture; the reason for the others is excessively high temperatures. The high temperatures encourage corrosion, which, in turn, tends to raise the temperature of the base. A simple method of minimizing these problems is to:

1. Switch the light to "off" and then play it safe by removing the plug or removing the appropriate fuse.
2. Scratch the metal contact at the center of the socket with a small screwdriver, an ice pick, or a sharp, pointed knife until appreciable amounts of the gray-black oxide have been removed to expose the original brass or silver color.
3. Wipe a thin film of petroleum jelly onto the threaded portion of the base of the bulb. Reinstall the bulb, and you should have a good, steady, rewarding glow.

Short Bulb Life in Certain Fixtures

The biggest light-bulb manufacturers have testified that their quality control is so tight and their knowledge of the thermodynamics and the kinetics of bulb filament decomposition is so extensive that they can predict bulb life to within a few hours. I'm impressed. But how come then that my last three-way bulb lasted exactly 2½ hours, and how come the bulbs in my trouble light have an average life of 15 hours (one lived exactly 3 seconds before dying a ghastly death on the basement floor); and how come the recessed lights in my kitchen would never qualify for a life insurance policy? The reason is that, while the bulb manufacturers may certainly understand bulbs and filaments, they certainly must not understand people and the demands we put on light bulbs.

My experience indicates that bulb life is shortened by:

1. Dropping. Wow, is it shortened!
2. Frequent on-off-on-off usage.
3. Frequent jiggling or bumping while on.
4. Overheating. This can result from poor lamp design ("contemporary" turret-type lamps are the worst) or from a poor connection in the lamp socket.

The only cause that can be readily minimized is the last. Follow the procedure for curing "the flickers" page 56.

A Light Switch or Lamp Switch Fails

When you think you've burned out a bulb, replace the bulb to no avail, check the fuses and find nothing but good health, the chances are that your switch has failed you. Replacement of switches is easy and safe if you follow the instructions in chapter 7.

For wall switches: See pages 68–70.

For lamp switches: See pages 75 and 86.

For switches on lamp cords: See pages 80–81.

The Doorbell Works Only on Halloween

If you have one of those doorbells that plays the "Minute Waltz" in 53 seconds while the unsuspecting visitor at your front door cowers in fear at the avalanche of sound he has just precipitated with his index finger, this section is not for you. Feel free to smugly stroll to your front door and play a little Chopin while everyone else reads what follows.

A doorbell system consists of three parts: the button, the bell (or chimes), and a transformer. A transformer is a voltage converter which, in this particular case, converts regular house current (115 volts) into about 12 volts, which does a better job on doorbells. You can picture the system like this:

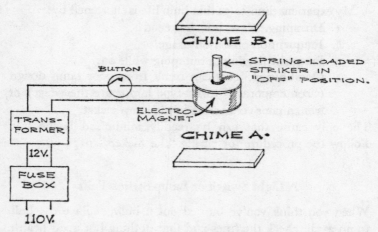

When the doorbell button is pressed, the loop is complete, current flows, the electromagnet yanks the striker rod down, and chime A goes BING; when the doorbell button is released, the current stops, the electromagnet goes dead, the striker rod, now under spring tension, flies upward, hitting chime B, which goes BONG.

Some doorbells have a second magnet and striker rod which is designed to hit chime A and miss chime B when a back doorbell is pushed.

Now that you know all this, the diagnosis of problems is easy. Ninety-five per cent of all door chime problems stem from two causes:

1. The switch that the doorbell button is supposed to close is corroded and fails (at least some of the time) to close that all-important electrical loop.

2. Little bits of grime, crud, and corrosion have deposited on the shaft of the striker rod, causing it to move so slowly (if at all) that it never gets to go BING and BONG any more.

Here's what you do:

1. With a fairly small screwdriver, loosen the screws[3] that hold the doorbell button in place. Then, after breaking through the layer of paint that is probably cementing it in place, slowly pull out the button assembly from its snuggly hole along with the two wires hooked to it. Using your screwdriver blade, touch a bare spot on one wire at the same time that you touch a bare spot on the other wire; hold it for

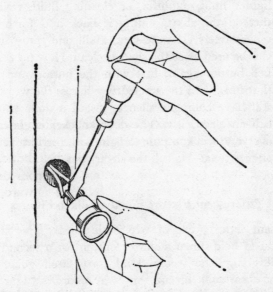

[3] Some simple buttons, like the one shown below, have no screws and are held in place simply by friction.

about 2 seconds, then remove the screwdriver. If
you hear your long-silent chimes or bell, you know
that a new switch will do the trick. (Chapter 5, pages
44–46, has a word of wisdom on this.

2. If your screwdriver didn't bring back the music,
remove the cover on your chime unit to expose its
sickly soul. You may have to loosen one screw at the
bottom center of the cover, but chances are that if
you simply swing the bottom of the cover away from
the wall, then lift up and out, you will have the
cover in your hands. Now locate the striker rod and
determine if it strikes easily or sluggishly. It's tempting
to oil this rod, but resist the temptation—oil is a
very temporary cure, because it soon becomes gummy
with more dirt and dust. Using a Q-Tip and some
lighter fluid, naphtha, or cleaning fluid, remove the
dirt on the shaft, sliding it back and forth until it
moves freely. If necessary, a silicone spray lubricant
can be used after the shaft is clean. Now try that doorbell button again, first with the button and then, if
that fails, with the screwdriver across the wires. If you
still have complete silence, install a door knocker or
call an electrician. The door knocker is cheaper, but
everyone will continue to fight with the button and get
angry at you—so call the electrician.

A Fluorescent Fixture Firmly Fails to Fluoresce

Fluorescent fixtures are of two basic kinds. The first kind
needs you to hold down a starter button for a second or two
to get it going; the second kind starts itself going (albeit
with an occasional hiccup or two before settling down)
when you flick a switch. Both types have three parts: a bulb,
a starter, and a transformer, or ballast. The starter on the

first type is activated by your finger and rarely malfunctions; the starter on the second type looks like a tiny tin can about an inch tall and burns out almost as frequently as the bulb does. Each bulb has its own starter.

A fluorescent bulb can fail to light for one of three reasons:

1. The bulb has burned out.
2. The starter has burned out.
3. The fixture is too cold (fluorescent lights will not ordinarily start at temperatures below 50° F).

If the bulb blinks on so much as once, the starter is working, and the bulb is worn out. If the bulb does absolutely nothing, either starter or bulb may be faulty, in which case I recommend trying a new starter (about $.25) first and a new bulb (over $1.00) second.

The bulb can be removed by grasping the tube at its center and twisting the cylinder (in either direction) exactly 90°. The tube should slip out of the socket. Reverse the procedure to install the new bulb.

I can hear you saying to me, "Great! It sounds easy to remove the bulbs once you get at them—but how in blazes do I get at the bulbs in my lamp?" I'm sorry to say that here you're on your own. Every fixture sports its own cover, and all I can suggest is that you should feel free to probe, pull, slide, unscrew, and press; the manufacturer wouldn't dare make it *too* difficult to get at the bulbs. In fact, I'll have to put you on your own in your hunt for the little tin can that is the starter—sometimes removing the bulb exposes the starter, and sometimes the starter is hidden behind another panel. Remove the starter by giving it a quarter turn in a counterclockwise direction (looking down at its top) and lifting it out of its socket.

Once in a great while a fluorescent fixture will begin to produce a horrendous odor and/or will drip drops of tar. This marks the demise of the ballast—its replacement is best left to an electrician. The smell will be sufficient to convince you to use other lighting until the transformer is replaced! A hum or buzz in a fluorescent fixture is also caused by a crotchety transformer. Such transformers are merely hypochondriacal—they're not really sick, and if you can stand their moaning, will live a long time.

As fluorescent bulbs age, they, like people, start up with greater and greater difficulty, flickering more and more before settling down to a healthy glow. A bulb that never gets out of the flickering stage, while not yet dead, is clearly ready for retirement and should be pensioned and replaced.

7

Electrical Repair Operations

I guess I dare tell you now: If you've figured out *what* to do, you're past the hard part. The *how to do it* part really is easy —easier than baking a cake, believe me.

There are four operations that are basic to all other operations: cutting a wire, stripping a wire, fastening a wire under a lug, and joining two wires.

CUTTING A WIRE

A slip-joint pliers usually *won't* do this job, but if the wire is a lamp cord, a pair of kitchen scissors will. Better yet, use a needlenose pliers with cutters, a tool that performs several hundred other jobs as well. Don't waste your money on one of those $.99 versions—expect a good one to cost $3.00 or $4.00. One chomp in the cutter of a quality pliers and your wire has been duly cut.

STRIPPING A WIRE

To connect two wires together, or to hook a wire to a fixture, the need is fortunately the same: about ½″ of bare wire.
To go

with a wire stripper, (see page 21) which has various size notches in the cutting edge allowing you to chomp (cutting only the insulation),

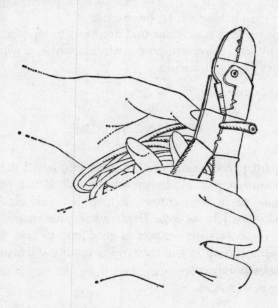

pull

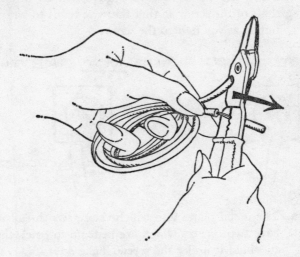

and get a cleanly stripped wire.

But, unless you expect to have electrical problems more than once a month, you can get away with using the same instrument that I used for years before my kids gave me a fancy wire stripper for Christmas—a kitchen knife. This versatile device works best when you cut quite gently through the insulation from four sides of the wire, then grab the almost loose piece of insulation, twist, and pull.

FASTENING A WIRE UNDER A LUG

Why they call them lugs is beyond me—they are nothing more than flat-headed screws which, when tightened down, hold the ends of wires firmly in place. They're found on nearly all plugs, wall outlets, and light switches; there's a right way and a wrong way to use them, and the right way is easier, so you may as well know it.

1. Make the tip of the wire go clockwise around the shaft of the screw so that the wire tends to wrap more tightly as you tighten the screw.

LIKE THIS: AND <u>NOT</u> LIKE THIS:

   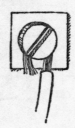

2. The metal plates into which the screws thread usually have two corners which are bent up to catch the wire and hold it under the screw. Take advantage of these when you wrap the wire.

3. If you're using multi-strand wire, give the wire end

a few twists after stripping it, like this,
to give it more cohesiveness when you tighten down on the screw.

JOINING TWO WIRES TOGETHER

If a friend asks if you have any wire nuts in your household, resist the temptation to ask her if she has any speedfreaks in hers. Her reference is to a handy gadget that joins the stripped ends of two or three wires together. It looks like a thimble for a girl who forgot to stop dieting, and it works without any tools at all, like this:

Twist the wires clockwise together slightly to give them a start. Thread the wire nut onto the twisted wires and keep turning until the nut is obviously tight and can't be pulled off.

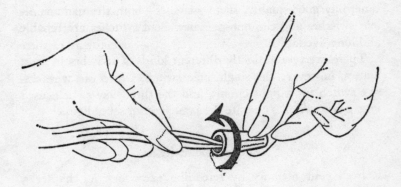

After you've twisted the wire nut tight, give each wire a fond farewell tug to be sure it's there to stay.

If this wire nut is too large, it will never tighten up, and you can continue turning forever. If you don't have a smaller nut, here's what to do:

1. If you can spare ½″ of wire, cut the twisted, stripped ends off.
2. Strip each wire back 1″ instead of the usual ½″.
3. Twist the stripped portion of the wires together, then bend the bare portion double.

4. Twist the wire nut onto this doubly thick wire.

If you have these four operations in hand, all the procedures in the rest of this chapter become duck soup.

REPLACING A WALL-MOUNTED LIGHT SWITCH

If you live in a development house, and your house is about eight years old, you may as well start buying your switches wholesale—sometime in the next two years almost every one of those switches will flop over one last time and die. (You didn't expect the builder to use the *best,* did you now?) This time, buy good-quality, silent switches—both the mercury silent switches and the non-mercury silent switches are reliable and long-lived.

There are two distinctly different kinds of switches in most houses, however: the single pole switch, which is the exclusive switch for a light circuit, and the three-way switch, used where two switches operate the same light or set of lights.[1]

Single Pole Switches

Refresh your memory by rereading exercise 5 in chapter 5 (see page 44).

1. Unscrew the fuse which controls the light to be repaired. If the light isn't working, and you're even slightly uncertain which fuse is the right one, turn off the entire electric supply by either removing the main fuse or pulling down the handle (if you have one) on the side of the box holding the main fuse.

2. Remove the cover plate by unscrewing the two screws that hold it on. (If you're working near a floor-

---

[1] A light that is operated by three switches involves two three-way switches and a four-way switch, which uses four wires and is slightly more complicated.

mounted warm-air register, better put a towel or newspaper over it in case you drop a screw.)

3. Remove the two screws that hold the switch in place and pull the switch out two or three inches.

4. Loosen the lugs on the old switch, and transfer the wires to the new switch. Either wire[2] can go to either lug in this case, but there is a top and a bottom to this switch: When the lever is down the word "off" should be visible.

5. Push the new switch back into place, making sure that the bare portions of the wires are touching neither each other nor the metal box.

6. Replace screws; put cover plate back on.

7. Occasionally you will find that the screws for the cover plate don't seem to be long enough to grab the threads of the holes in the new switch, or sometime you may discover that the new switch barely sticks out through the cover plate. Cure either problem by loosening the screws holding the switch to the wall by two or three turns. Then replace the cover plate and try again. If the cover plate isn't straight, simply loosen the cover plate screws a couple of turns, straighten things up, and tighten them down again.

8. Turn the power back on. Reset electric clocks.

Three-Way Switches

A three-way switch requires just an ounce of extra care, because it uses three wires:

[2] Usually you will find the switch attached to two wires—one black, one white. Occasionally, three wires will be attached—two black, one red; simply connect the black wires to one lug and the red wire to another. You may find that your wires connect to your switch simply by being poked into small holes in the back of the switch. To remove a wire from a switch like that, just push a small screwdriver into the slot next to the hole and pull out the wire. New switches may have three such holes. Examine them carefully and observe that two of the holes are connected to each other. Use these two holes for the two black wires (if there are, in fact, two blacks and a red).

1. Turn off either the circuit fuse or the main house fuse as in step 1, page 68.
2. Remove cover plate and the screws holding the faulty switch just as in steps 2 and 3, pages 68–69.
3. When you pull out the old switch and its wires, notice that the wires are black, white, and red, and that the black wire is attached to a lug at the top of the switch (of course, your switch may be upside down, but that doesn't matter here.[3]
4. Install the new switch, which may look slightly different, but will have two lugs at the bottom (for the red wire and the white wire) and one lug at the top (for the black wire). Unlike the single pole switch, there is really no right side up or upside down for this switch; so red and white at bottom and black at top is just as happy an arrangement.
5. Replace switch and cover plate just as in steps 5, 6, 7, and 8 of the single switch (page 69).

REPLACING A WALL OUTLET

The gadget to ask for in a hardware store is a "duplex receptacle." And as if that's not enough, the salesman will ask you, "Lady, you want grounded or ungrounded?" Don't stutter; just say "yes" and let him do a little stuttering. Better yet, look at the outlet you intend to replace before you make your trip to the hardware store. If it looks like this,

---

[3] Not all electricians follow the same convention on this, and you may find your switch hooked to a black and red at the top (or bottom) and a red at the other end. Whatever you find, remember the combination you found and duplicate it on the new switch.

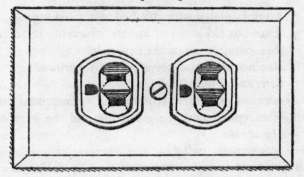

you want a grounded receptacle; but if it looks like this,

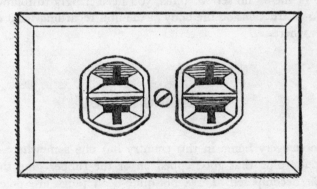

it's an ungrounded receptacle that you want.

The grounded receptacle can be replaced in the following manner:

1. Remove the appropriate circuit fuse or kill the power to the entire house as described in step 1, page 68.
2. Remove the cover plate (only one screw is holding it).
3. Remove the two screws that hold the receptacle in place, and pull receptacle plus wires out of its box.
4. Observe that there are three wires involved:
   A black (or red) wire attached to a brass-colored lug.
   A white insulated wire attached to a silver-colored lug.

An uninsulated wire attached to a green lug.

5. Take out old and put in new, observing to reproduce these connections on the new unit.
6. Replace unit and cover plate by performing steps 5, 6, 7, and 8 on page 69.

An ungrounded receptacle requires the same procedure with the single exception that the green lug and the bare copper wire will be absent.

Very convenient switches and receptacles are available which don't use lugs, but are connected by poking the right wires into the right holes. If you find that you have purchased one of these "no screw" units, you need merely to follow the clear instructions on the body of the unit regarding what color goes where.

REPLACING A PLUG

Almost every home in this country has one somewhere—the bakelite plug that got stepped on or the rubber plug that is 60% decomposed. These not-quite-dead plugs are potential disaster units and should be replaced immediately, if not sooner. Do the following:

1. Pull the plug from the outlet.
2. If the cord is still good, snip the cord about 2 inches from the offending plug.
3. If the cord is standard lamp cord, and the fixture uses no more than 300 watts, install one of those dandy "clip-on" plugs that have taken all the sweat out of plug switching.

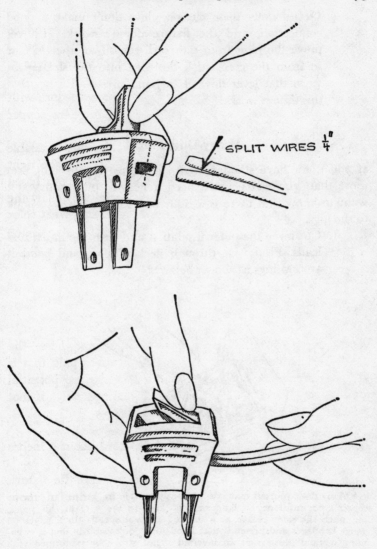

SPLIT WIRES $\frac{1}{4}''$

4. Occasionally these clip-on plugs don't make a good connection, and the fixture doesn't work. Just remove the plug from the cord, cut off another ¼″ or so from the cord, stick the cord into the slot again, press that lever down hard, and presto—I'll bet that this time it works!

Heavy-Duty Plugs

If you don't have standard lamp cord, or if your unit uses more than 300 watts, you'll need a heavier plug and you'll want to know that there *is* a right way for the wires to hook to the lugs.

1. Cut away the outer insulation and strip the individual leads. Feed wire through neck of plug and bend it around lugs as shown below: [4]

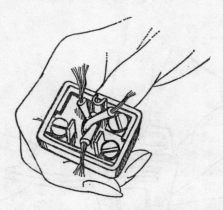

---

[4] Many do-it-yourself manuals, obviously written by purists for gung-ho repair types insist on an Underwriters' knot in the wire at this point, for much the same reason as a first-aid manual spends three pages on gauze bandages and pretends that Band-Aids don't exist or that a swimming manual insists that an inverted breast stroke be performed with a nice, symmetrical frog kick, but never mentions that you go faster if you contaminate the frog kick with about 15% scissors kick. The fact is that most of the repairmen I know don't bother with an Underwriters' knot.

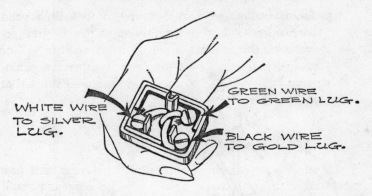

WHITE WIRE
TO SILVER
LUG.

GREEN WIRE
TO GREEN LUG.

BLACK WIRE
TO GOLD LUG.

2. Make sure that there are no stray strands of wire free to reach the other lug or stray wires from the other lug. If there are, snip them off.

3. Slide cardboard cover plate over your wiring job.

REPLACING A DEFECTIVE LAMP SOCKET WITH SWITCH

Did I just see you turn that table lamp off by pulling the plug out of the wall? Shame on you—when it's so easy to replace that lamp socket with the broken switch! (What, pray tell, would you have done if the switch died in the OFF position?)

Suddenly your experience from exercise 2 (page 37) is ready to pay off big:

1. Pull the plug—the one on the lamp cord that's in the wall outlet.

2. Remove light bulb and shade. (The shade removal isn't imperative—just convenient.)

3. Use the strength of both hands and press, with your thumb, inward and upward on the spot on the barrel that says PRESS.

4. Remove the metal barrel and the cardboard sleeve found just inside the barrel.

5. Suddenly the "guts" of the lamp socket is flopping loosely in front of you, waiting to be removed by loosening the two lugs.

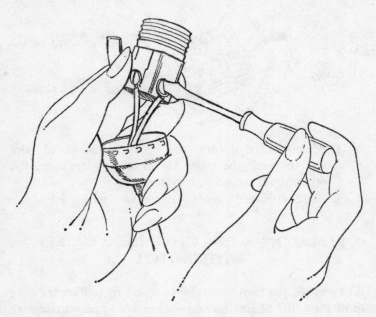

6. The new replacement (see page 86 for the choices you have) comes complete with the bottom piece, which you probably won't have to use. Set this piece aside. Get your hands on the new "guts" and get it into its floppy place by hooking in the two wires. (Which wire goes to which lug doesn't matter.)
7. Slide the new cardboard sleeve into place.
8. Snap the new barrel into place by getting its corrugated edges inside the rim of the old base that you didn't replace, then pushing down until you hear a solid, reassuring click as each side snaps in place.
9. Check the base's grab on the barrel by trying to yank it back out (*without* pressing on press!). If it's in there to stay, your plug-pulling days are over.

Turret-type Desk Lamps and Pole Lamps

Although I'm less than enthusiastic about this type of lamp, they're cheap, attractive, plentiful, and prone to problems, so I had better tell you how to repair them. The most common style is a lamp with a switch at the back end of the turret:

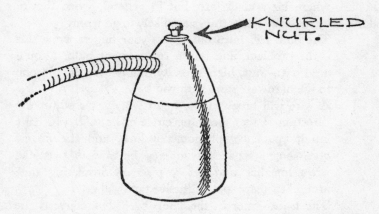

KNURLED NUT.

The switch may be either push-button or rotary—both make it easy for you to burn your hand on the overheated lamp shade (which is the first reason for my unenthusiasm).

The secret to disassembling this kind of lamp lies in (a) patience and (b) getting the knurled nut loose. Use a pliers to get the nut started; try not to leave any tooth marks from the pliers, although this is tough. Then pull the socket out of the lamp shade, feeding wire through the innards of the lamp as necessary (and this is the second reason for my unenthusiasm—sometimes it's tough to feed that wire!). After you get the socket out and have freed the two wires, take the socket to your hardware store and get an exact match for the old socket. In goes the new socket by reversing the procedure you just followed.

Sometimes these turret lamps get disgustingly loose on their adjustable, rotatable arms and won't stay pointed where you want them pointed. Cure this by getting a fairly hefty screwdriver and tightening every screw at every elbow in sight.

High-Intensity Desk Lamps

Those neat little high-intensity lamps are just great for catching up on your reading next to a snoring husband who wants it dark where his eyeballs are, but in general, when they're done, they're done. Three things are likely to go wrong:

1. The bulb will burn out. Cross your fingers, hope this is the problem, and buy a replacement bulb. (You'll need a 12-watt, high-intensity bulb—take the old one to the hardware store with you.)

2. A wire will break at the point where you adjust the direction of that gleaming circle of light. If you have infinite patience, phenomenal luck, and the fingers of a shoemaker's elf, you *may* be able to twist the wires together and get a piece of insulating tape around the bare spot (adhesive tape will do).

3. The transformer in the lamp base that converts the 115 volts to 12 volts for a bright, yet long-lived filament will burn out. Just face it, these lamps weren't made to be repaired, particularly if the transformer has failed. Throw it away.

TIGHTENING UP LAMPS THAT HAVE THE SHAKES

The socket feels like it should be screwed on more tightly; you can't unscrew the bulb without holding the socket to keep it from turning too; the whole lamp feels just a little as if it had lost its starch. The ailment is irritating, but the cure is easy as soon as you discover how lamps are put together:

Most lamps are nothing more than a threaded hollow shaft with a socket screwed on at the top, a fancy doodad (and that doodad is what cost you the $89—the working parts of the lamp didn't cost more than $2.00) to cover up the shaft and provide a base to make the shaft stand up straight, and finally a nut fastened to the bottom of the shaft. A diagram will say it better:

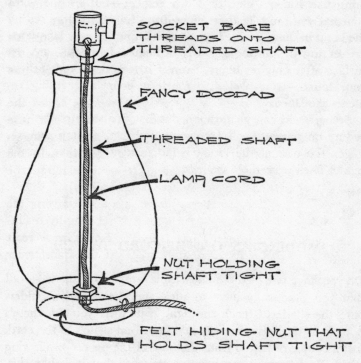

SOCKET BASE
THREADS ONTO
THREADED SHAFT

FANCY DOODAD

THREADED SHAFT

LAMP CORD

NUT HOLDING
SHAFT TIGHT

FELT HIDING NUT THAT
HOLDS SHAFT TIGHT

Now that you know that every lamp's working parts are worth about the same $2.00, you, too, can be incensed at lamps selling for $100 and more. That fancy cover can't be worth all *that* much!

You can easily see why a lamp loosens up; for some reason or other, that bottom nut starts to unscrew itself, getting looser and looser with every little vibration that the lamp undergoes.

How can you cure it? *Not* by just screwing the bulb and socket until they're tight—you twist the wire dangerously that way. You can do one of two things:

First, you can carefully remove the felt that covers the lamp base, thereby uncovering the nut so you can tighten it. Cement the felt back onto the base of the lamp with something like Elmer's glue or Duco cement—but let me warn you that you must let these glues dry a full day before setting the lamp in place again. I once ruined a nearly new lacquered dresser top by putting a newly cemented felt base onto the surface after only six hours. Even if it feels dry, don't believe your touch—wait twelve to fourteen hours after using cements like Duco.

Second, you can go through the first five steps of the procedure on pages 75–76 (replacing a defective lamp socket). When the base of the socket is independent of wires, turn it tight.[5] Then reassemble the light.

ADDING AN ON-THE-CORD SWITCH

Do you have one of those large table lamps with shade so tall that you practically have to stick your head and shoulders onto the shade to reach the light switch? If you do, there's hope in sight. You can easily add an off-on switch to the cord, just a couple of inches from the base of the people-swallowing lamp. Rather small, unobtrusive switches that look like this, page 81, and carry 600 watts are available in either brown or white and are so easy to install it's almost embarrassing. Here's all you do:

[5] In some lamp socket bases there is a "set screw" screwed through the socket base to keep it from turning. Loosen it a turn or two, turn the socket base tight and retighten the screw.

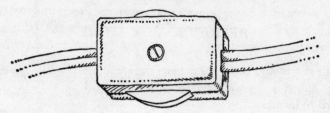

1. Open the switch by unscrewing the screw.
2. Cut *just one* of the two wires in the lamp cord at the point where you wish the switch to be. Don't even bother to strip the wires.

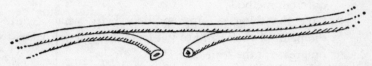

3. Lay the wires in the bottom half of the switch (the half without the wheel) like this,

4. Lay the other half on top and squeeze down. Judiciously placed prongs will pierce the insulation and make the necessary contact (just as in the quickie clip-on lamp plug I recommended).

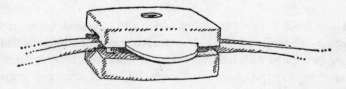

5. Replace the screws and tighten them.

REPLACING A STOVE OR
REFRIGERATOR LIGHT

Both stoves and refrigerators use the same light bulb—it's usually called a 15-watt refrigerator bulb and may be a little hard to locate.

Stoves usually have a threaded glass globe over the bulb—grab it tightly and give it the catsup-bottle loosening treatment. It will occasionally be quite resistant to your attempt to unscrew it, in which case you:

1. Look at it carefully to see if it's held in place by some different method;
2. Give the thing an appropriately hefty whack with the palm of your hand to jolt loose the years of baked-on grease at the seams.

Once you get the glass cover out, you'll not be able to resist the desire to clean it. (Oven cleaner is fine.) Just don't bake or broil anything until you get it back in place.

Refrigerator manufacturers are so clever and sneaky about how they assemble the cover plate over the light that all I can tell you is to push, push, lift, wiggle, and slide until it comes off. There may even be a couple of Phillips head screws to loosen.

INSTALLING A WALL-MOUNTED
DIMMER SWITCH

If you limit yourself to lights which are operated by a single switch, it's really remarkably easy. After you choose your dimmer (see page 87) remove your old light switch by following the complete procedure on page 68, with one exception: When you are ready to hook the wires to the dimmer, you will have to join wires to wires instead of wires to lugs, so you will have to use the technique described on page 66 instead. You'll undoubtedly find wire nuts supplied in the dimmer box just for the occasion. When you push the dimmer unit into the receptacle box, you may find the space a little cramped. However, given a little patience and ingenuity, I'm almost sure you will successfully stuff it all in far enough to get the cover plate (use the same cover plate) back on again.

8

Electrical Parts

WHAT TO BUY

Even though you have been buying your light bulbs in the hardware store, as I suggested in chapter 3, and have cased the electrical-parts section several times now, you are not yet, I know, exactly a connoisseur of switches, sockets, and plugs. Hence, the next few pages contain short bursts of advice to the neophyte electrical-parts shopper.

Buy Safe. UL stands for Underwriters' Laboratory, a private, nongovernment, nationally recognized testing laboratory financed by the electrical manufacturing industry. The UL seal on an electrical part is no guarantee that it's a good buy, convenient to use, easy to install, or impervious to the vicious attacks of your German shepherd, but it is a guarantee that, when properly used, it's safe. Make it an inviolable rule that every electrical part you buy be UL approved. Generally, hardware stores are very conscientious about handling only UL-approved parts; the places to be cautious are the discount drug stores and grocery stores.

Fluorescent bulbs: Fluorescent bulbs come in various lengths and wattages, but it's not necessary to measure the length of your tube, since the wattage is proportional to the length. For example, all 2′ tubes are 20 watts and all 4′ tubes (they're actually about an inch shorter than these nominal lengths) are 40 watts. You'll find the manufacturer, the color, and the wattage printed on the tube at one end.

Fixtures usually come equipped with "cool white" bulbs, but I recommend replacing them with "warm white" bulbs. They cost no more, deliver just as much light (there was a time when they didn't), and give a much better rendition of colors together with more flattering skin tone appearance.

Plugs: If you walk into a hardware store and ask for a plug, the salesman is likely to look you quizzically in the eyes and say, "Male or female?" Don't blush—he's not expressing doubts as to your sexual persuasion, but merely wants to know whether you want a plug that looks

...LIKE THIS: OR THIS:

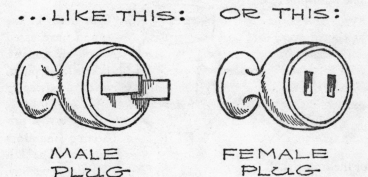

MALE PLUG   FEMALE PLUG

Almost invariably you'll be able to smile and coolly answer, "a male plug, of course." He'll wonder for the rest of the day whether he should have explained his question to you.

Don't buy a plug that isn't easy to grab and pull out of the outlet; such plugs encourage people to yank the cord instead of the plug.

If you're using an outlet behind a hutch (or similar piece of furniture) and would like that hutch to be as close to the wall as possible, the plug for you is available; it's no larger than a man's watch and requires only about ½" clearance because it sends the wire out the side.

The easy-to-attach "clip on" plug mentioned on page 72 is fine for lamps and an occasional small appliance that can be wired by lamp cord, but they just won't work on anything but lamp cord and should *not* be used on appliances such as toasters, waffle irons, steam irons, and electric fry pans.

"Bare bulb" ceramic light fixtures: of the sort found in most cellars (before conversion to clubrooms), are available, not only with pull chain switch, but also with a plug outlet next to the bulb socket, for only a few cents more. To the extent that your cellar is short of outlets (most cellars are), this addition is worth the extra cost.

Standard lamp socket switches are of two types:
The push-pull type:

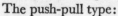

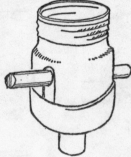

or the rotary shaft type:

My experience is that the rotary shaft switches live longer.

Dimmer switches are of two types. The first works just like most "on-volume" switches on table model radios—a twist to the left makes the light dimmer and dimmer until finally, with a click, it's off. The second is more expensive and, while it dims similarly with a twist, it turns on and off simply with a push. In my opinion, the added convenience of the second type is worth the extra cost.

Also available is a lamp socket dimmer switch which accomplishes with a single-wattage light bulb what a three-way lamp does with a dual filament bulb. These switches aren't cheap, but they are just as easy to install as a standard switch and should pay for themselves in light bulb savings after about three years' use.

Fuses, lifesavers that they are, are a nuisance when they blow because, through no fault of the poor dying fuse, our human nature is such that we don't keep an emergency supply. If your human nature is more this way than most people, you may find it worth buying a fuse-shaped circuit breaker that never burns out, but clicks off instead, simultaneously extending a little button through its face which merely requires a push for restoration of current. They cost enough that you can replace many fuses for less money, but the convenience may be worth the difference.

9

Getting to Know Your Plumbing

This is a get-acquainted chapter on programmed plumbing, designed as a "do" and not just a "read" experience. Literally, I want you to walk through the house following the instructions below so that when the inevitable plumbing emergency materializes, you will neither feel nor be at its mercy. So, off to a guided tour of your water works in which you'll tap the secrets of the toilet and tub and bare the behavior of the basin. Take this book in your hot hand and let's go! The bathroom is a good place to begin.

THE LAVATORY

Look for cut-off valves on the wall below the basin. You should be able to trace the connections from the cold and hot water faucets to wall cut-off. Turn (by hand) the handle of the hot water valve clockwise until it is closed. Try turning on the hot water faucet. Repeat with the cut-off and cold water faucet. Finally leave both valves wide open. If you find no cut-off valves, look for them in the cellar almost directly beneath the lavatory.

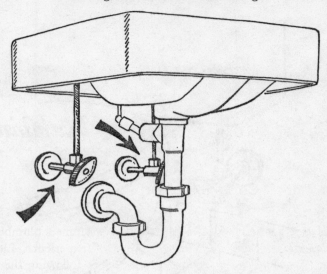

Close the lavatory drain and fill the bowl, but don't turn off the water. It shouldn't run over because there is an *internal overflow* built into all lavatories: the obvious hole (plain or with grill) facing you at the back of the bowl and somewhat below the level of the rim. But many bowls have their overflow hidden under an overhanging lip inside the front rim. These overflow holes have to be plugged up when you are using a "plumber's friend" to unstop the drain (see page 121).

Under the lavatory is a U-shaped chrome-plated "trap." "The trap trick" (page 122) will tell you why it's there.

THE TOILET

There won't be a hot water line to the toilet—only a cold one. Its cut-off valve should be behind it on the wall. Turn it clockwise until it's closed.

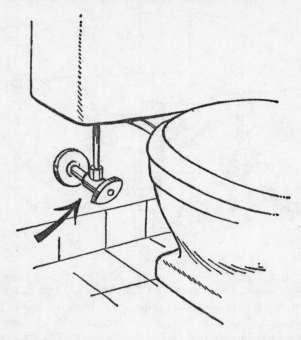

With both hands (one under each end) grasp and lift the ceramic lid off the water tank and place it carefully on newspaper or a bath mat. Now, watch what happens in the tank when you flush the toilet.

When the toilet tank is emptied, use the diagram to identify every part of the toilet mechanism. Even if your toilet mechanism differs in some details from the diagram, you'll recognize its three basic parts: At the center front, attached to the exterior handle, is the flush valve unit; at the far left is the water inlet valve unit, to which the float arm is connected; between them stands the overflow pipe, with the bowl refill pipe pointed at its open end.

After identifying on your toilet each labeled part on the diagram, move the float arm up and down with your hand and observe the motion at the top of the inlet valve unit.

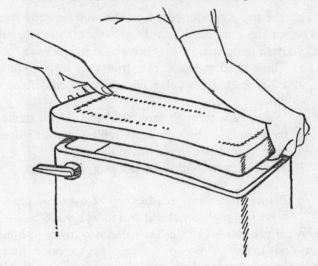

Notice that as the float is raised, a small plunger at the top of the inlet valve is pushed down. This plunger moves down until its bottom surface closes a hole through which the water is entering, stopping the water. The plunger, you'll notice, could be easily removed by removing one or two screws on the float arm mechanism and pulling the plunger straight up.

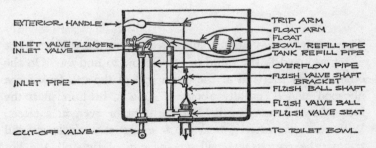

Depress the exterior handle a few times, observing its action of raising the flush valve ball, or "flush ball." The flush ball shaft should slide smoothly and easily through the bracket.

With the top still removed, turn the water supply back on and watch the tank fill. Flush the toilet a couple more times, until you can understand each operational step below:

1. Flush ball lifts. Water runs from tank through bowl.
2. Float falls. Inlet valve plunger rises, and inlet valve opens.
3. Water runs through tank refill pipe to fill tank. Water also runs through bowl refill pipe, into overflow pipe, and thence to the rim of the bowl.
4. Float rises as tank fills, pushing inlet valve plunger down.
5. Before water level reaches top of overflow pipe, inlet valve is completely closed and toilet turns off.

Now, if you have read this far without actually opening the toilet and following the procedure, I guarantee that you won't know enough when toilet fixing time comes. Understand that toilet *now* to make the repair instructions in chapter 10 understandable *then*.

THE CUT-OFF VALVES ON OTHER FIXTURES

Tub

There may or may not be cut-off valves for the cold and hot water supplied to the tub, but here's how to find out. On the other side of the wall at the drain end of the tub look for a plywood panel (usually about $1\frac{1}{2}' \times 2'$), held in place by four screws. It may be behind the door or even in a closet. With your screwdriver, turn the screws counterclockwise and remove the panel: you will see the end of the tub, the hot and cold water pipes (with or without cut-off valves) and the drain pipe. If you see no valves, look directly under the tub in the basement. Even if there aren't any cut-off valves, you can still work on the tub faucets (see page 92) by cutting off the main house valve (see below). Replace the wooden panel and screws.

Shower

If there's no cut-off in the basement, the main water valve must be closed to change washers (see page 99) in the shower fixture.

Kitchen Sink

Look in the cabinet directly below the sink for the hot and cold water cut-offs. There may or may not be any. If not, look in the basement. Again, if none are provided, the main cut-off will serve to isolate the sink.

Dishwasher

There'll be only a hot water line to the dishwasher. If you have a basement, go down and look for the valve directly below the dishwasher. If none, back to the main cut-off again.

Laundry Tub

The hot and cold water lines will come down from the ceiling above and almost certainly no cut-offs will be provided. Again, use the main cut-off.

THE WATER METER

Although it may be inside on your basement wall nearest the street, it may also be located in front of your house between the sidewalk and the curb in a cylindrical hole with a heavy round cover. If the meter is outside, your water line will run directly from it, and its location gives a clue to where in your house you may find the main cut-off valve.

THAT MAIN CUT-OFF

It controls all water coming in, and, as I said, is usually located quite near where the water line enters the house. It will most likely have a round handgrip and operate normally: counterclockwise to open; clockwise to close. Exert this new-found power you have over all things aqueous by closing the main valve and then opening the faucet—say, in the laundry tub or kitchen sink—to be sure that what you found is really the main valve. But don't forget to reopen it before you try to take a bath.

It's just possible that somewhere there may be a secondary cut-off which controls the water in a specific portion of your house. See if you can find one. Look for another plywood panel in a wall or ceiling, possibly in a closet or in a down-stairs bathroom.

A PLUMBING GAME

Time: Sunday morning—two o'clock.

Situation: You've just come home from a real bang-up evening—a fabulous dinner, theater and party afterward. You kick off your shoes and go to the basement because, subconsciously, you think you left some clothes in the washer. Down the steps you go, and as your foot hits the basement floor—SPLASH!!!

NOW—in the security of your non-flooded basement—figure out what you would do in that situation. The chapter you've just walked through and chapter 12 should allow you to sleep soundly once again.

In fact, the next three chapters will supply insurance and assurance that you are ready to cope not only with the common plumbing nuisances but also with those previously devastating emergencies which made you feel so helpless.

10

The Chinese Water Torture

Economically, emotionally and ecologically speaking, a drip is bad, bad, bad. Water leaks (drip) can either (drip) drive you (drip) out of (drip) your mind (drip) or (drip) flood you out of house and home. A single faucet dripping only 30 drops per minute uses over 50 gallons of water in a month, and the faucet running in a stream so tiny it breaks up into droplets on the way down can waste over 2,000 gallons in a month. However large the local supply and whatever your water rate is, that's no drop in anybody's bucket.

So, grab a screwdriver and a crescent wrench and come with me to the nearest leaky faucet. *But first,* close the main cut-off valve or the cut-off valve where the drip is (see page 94).

FAUCETS—LAVATORY, TUB, KITCHEN, AND OUTSIDE

Wherever you find them, faucets are faucets; in spite of how fancy or plain on the outside, they are all sisters under the skin.

On the lavatory, kitchen sink, and tub faucets just below or behind the handle there will be a chrome housing, usually held in place by a set screw or a flat chrome nut.

The Handle

First turn on the faucet about three-quarters of the way. No water? Good. You did close the cut-off valve. Leave the faucet open. If there's a housing, remove the handle first.

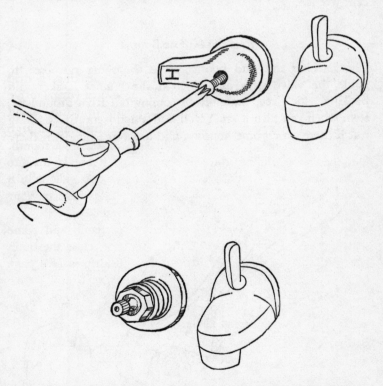

The handle is invariably held on by a screw which may or may not be covered by a snap-on or screw-on cap (the edges will be serrated) labeled "C" or "H." Put all screws and parts in a cup for safekeeping unless you would like to do "the trap trick" (see page 122) to remove those which fall in the drain. After you've removed the screw holding it, the handle may be stubborn about coming off. Tap it on one side and then the other from *underneath* or *behind* with a piece of wood or your screwdriver handle.

If there's a housing, remove it by loosening the set screw (counterclockwise) or by taping the chrome nut (to prevent scarring it) and turning it counterclockwise with the crescent wrench.

Packing Nut or Bonnet

The packing nut and bonnet serve the same purpose: to guide the valve stem and to hold the bonnet washer and packing which keep water from coming out from around the stem when you turn it on. You'll find a nondecorative packing nut if there's a chrome housing, and a chrome bonnet if there

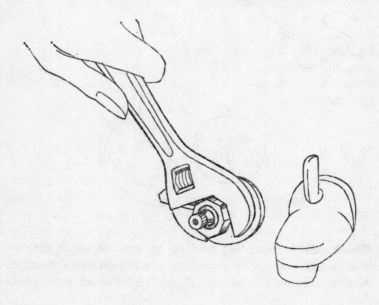

isn't; or the whole fixture may be made of brass if it's outside or in the basement.

Loosen the packing nut or chrome bonnet (tape wrapped)

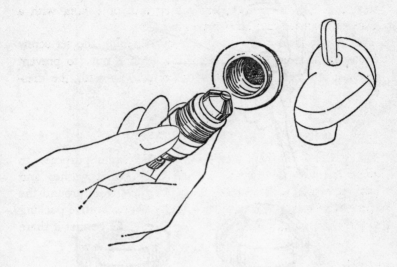

by turning counterclockwise while you hold the stem to keep it from turning. It is not necessary to take it off the stem. With a turn by hand the whole valve stem should now come out easily.

Valve Stem Washer

The heart of the system, that little round, black or oval washer held on the end of the valve stem by a brass screw determines whether there will or won't be a drip. The turn of the handle clockwise cuts off the water by forcing the washer against the valve seat. If the washer is brittle, or broken, or rough, or if the valve seat has been gouged and doesn't fit the washer—drip, drip, drip—or worse.

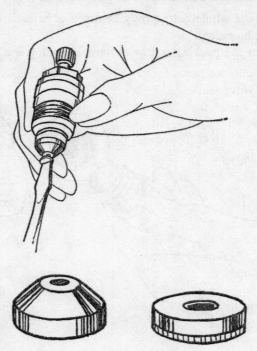

There will be a number on the back of the old washer (0, ¼, ¼R, ⅜, etc.)—but it may be illegible. If so, take the valve stem to the hardware store and make sure that the washers you buy fit exactly into the little depression on its end. Insert the washer (rounded side out) and the brass retaining screw. Write down the washer number and tape it out of sight nearby. Maybe when you go to the hardware store you'd prefer to get a package of washers of assorted sizes. It's a good buy, since all your faucets won't require the same size washer.

Valve Seat

With your finger feel the beveled edge of the valve seat opening. It should be smooth and even. If it's not, you can buy a tool to resmooth the valve seat or you can replace it, depending upon its type. By all means, replace it if you have the chance. Look carefully at it. The hole the water comes through may be hexagonal or it may be square. This means that the valve seat can be unscrewed (counterclockwise) and replaced using the correct size "hex" or "Allen" wrench (see page 22) or a square wrench, all of which are readily available. Take the old valve seat to the hardware store and get an identical one. Screw it in and tighten. If your valve seat does not have a hexagonal or square hole and is not replaceable, resort to the resmoothing tool, but it's a last resort, since it's a mean job to do satisfactorily. Follow the directions on the package.

Replace the valve stem with a turn to the right (but not quite all the way) then tighten the packing nut or bonnet snugly. Next, the housing (if any) and handle. Try opening and closing the faucet; it should operate smoothly. Close it and turn on the cut-off valve.

Bonnet Leak

If there's a leak around the bonnet or housing, try tightening the bonnet or packing nut. It may be necessary to replace the packing and/or bonnet washer. Neither presents a problem.

Faucets—Single-Lever Type

Your lavatory or kitchen sink may have *one* control handle for *hot and cold* water, and that's a different sort of animal from the usual faucet. The control section of the most common-type single-lever mixing faucet consists of a cylindrical cartridge which can be replaced easily when necessary.[1]

[1] There are a number of other less common types of single level faucets, at least one of which has clear, printed repair directions (with drawings) for the homeowner stashed away in a little covered compartment on the back of the unit.

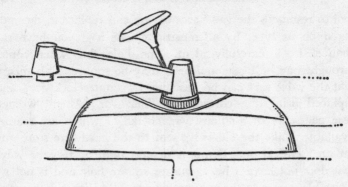

Faced with any dripping single-lever faucet, try this first: repeatedly and vigorously turn the handle to full on and to full off in the hot and in the cold positions; next, with the water still on, rock the handle between the extreme hot and cold positions. Frequently this will dislodge a speck of grit responsible for the drip.

If the drip persists, replace the cartridge. Here's how:

After closing the cut-off valve, remove the spout by loosening with your fingers the knurled nut at its base. (If it's too tight for fingers, wrap a layer of adhesive tape around the knurled nut and grasp it with slip-joint pliers.) After you lift

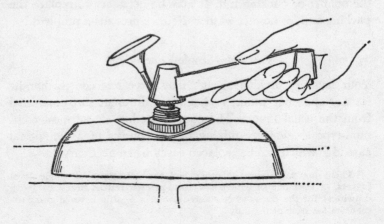

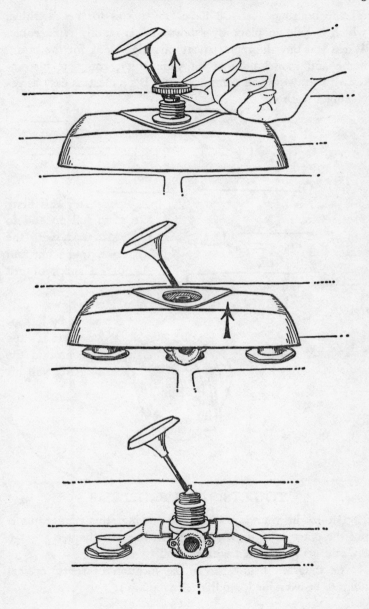

off the housing, you will have easy access to the cartridge, which is held in place by screws and is readily replaceable. When you buy the replacement cartridge (look for the brand name and model number on your unit), complete instructions (a drawing will come with it). It's almost as easy as replacing a washer.

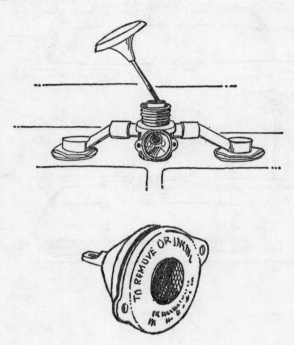

TOILETS WITH PROBLEMS

If a toilet in your house is misbehaving, this paragraph is not the place to begin reading. Turn back to chapter 9, page 89, and get acquainted with the toilet.

The diagram below shows the location of seven critical items to be examined, modified, or replaced:

1. The flush valve shaft bracket
2. The flush valve ball
3. The float arm
4. The float
5. The inlet valve plunger
6. The top of the overflow pipe
7. The water supply pipe

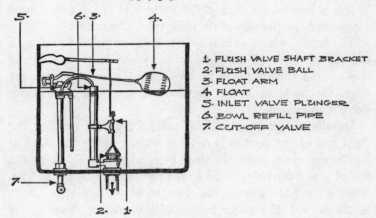

1. FLUSH VALVE SHAFT BRACKET
2. FLUSH VALVE BALL
3. FLOAT ARM
4. FLOAT
5. INLET VALVE PLUNGER
6. BOWL REFILL PIPE
7. CUT-OFF VALVE

The following instructions for curing the ills of a toilet will refer to the numbered locations of this diagram.

Toilet Runs Full Speed Until Exterior Handle Is Jiggled

The cause is undue friction in the flush valve ball lifting mechanism, usually at location 1. If flush valve shaft bracket does not guide the flush ball directly onto the center of the flush valve seat, of if the flush ball shaft is bent, correct the situation by moving the bracket (it's held by one large screw) or by straightening the shaft.

It also helps to cut off the water supply, flush the toilet, and, after drying the flush ball shaft, to spray it with silicone spray lubricant. Don't forget to turn the water supply on again.

Toilet Never Turns Off Completely

There are two possible causes for a toilet to run constantly: Water is leaving the tank either by way of the overflow pipe (location 6), or by way of the flush valve (location 2).

To decide which exit is being used, examine location 6, the top of the overflow pipe. If the water level rises all the way to the top of the pipe and begins to trickle over the edge, the problem is that the float is not closing the water valve soon enough.

Usually the problem can be cured simply by bending the right end of the float arm down a little, making the bend at location 3. Just grab the float arm with one hand to the left of 3 and the other hand to the right of 3, and bend. Stop turning up your nose at the thought of putting your hands in the water! The water in the tank is just as clean as the water in the lavatory. If it seems objectionably dirty to you, feel free to scour it as you would a sink, cutting off the water supply and flushing the toilet to empty the tank, and opening the water supply tap to rinse the tank after washing.

If bending the float arm doesn't solve the problem, it may be that the float arm doesn't float well enough because water has leaked into it. If the float (location 4) floats with less than 70% above the surface, check for water in the float by closing the water supply tape, flushing the toilet to empty the tank, and shaking the ball up and down. The sound of water sloshing around inside marks the end of your quest— the hardware store will have a replacement for you. Remove the old one, unscrewing it by hand.

If the float arm is quite bent, the float contains no water, and the toilet still overfills, it's time to replace the inlet valve plunger (location 5). Examine the arm that holds the plunger in place, decide which screws to remove to free the plunger, remove the screws, and lift out the plunger. Take the plunger to the hardware store; chances are good that you can get exact replacements for the rubber parts of the plunger. Don't be surprised if the new parts cause the plunger to fit tighter.

If parts are unavailable, you can buy (for about $5.00) a replacement for the entire inlet pipe and inlet valve unit. Economical, reliable, plastic units that do not need a separate float are available.

It is possible that the toilet may be leaking through the flush valve (location 2) instead of the overflow pipe. If the water in your tank never rises to the top of the overflow pipe (location 3), but the toilet still leaks, check the flush valve ball to make sure that it seats in the center of its hole. Check the valve seat to make sure the surface is smooth, smoothing it with a steel wool pad if necessary. If the flush ball feels rough or ragged, or is torn or irregular in any way, it can be removed by holding the shaft and turning the flush ball *clockwise*. The hardware store will have a replacement.

Toilet Is Unduly Noisy

A noisy toilet can often be quieted by partially closing the toilet's water cut-off valve, slowing the rate of water flow. Of course, the toilet will take longer to fill as a result.

Water Shoots Out of Inlet Valve When Toilet Fills

Many toilet inlet valve units are designed to allow some water to spray harmlessly past the inlet valve plunger (location 5) while it's filling. Occasionally a unit will allow water to spray upward with enough force to hit the toilet cover and leak out. In this case, remove the plunger as just described, take it to a hardware store, and get replacements for the rubber sleeve or sleeves around the circumference of the plunger. (Some plungers have sides which are grooved to accept little rubber doughnuts called "O" rings; these are also available at hardware stores.)

Toilet Is Clogged

This problem is quite different from those being described here, and is covered thoroughly in chapter 12.

Toilet Leaks, but Is Quiet About It

Most leaking toilets emit a hiss or a whistle or a squeak, but occasionally a unit will waste great quantities of water in complete silence. If you suspect that your toilet is a sneaky leaker, add ink or food coloring to the water in the tank before retiring some evening. Colored water in the bowl the next morning indicates that it is, in fact, leaking.

Pipe Between Cut-Off Valve and Toilet Springs a Leak (Location 7)

Close the cut-off valve and loosen the nuts at both ends of the pipe. At the top of the pipe there will be two nuts; loosen the lower one, holding the upper one stationary. Take the pipe and the nuts with you to the hardware store for replacement.

TOILET SEATS

The paint's flaking and discolored or the wood's cracked so that you have to keep the lid down to avoid embarrassment when company comes? Five minutes and a few dollars for a new seat and lid and you have it made. Wood, plastic, plastic-covered wood, plain, carved, eagle-creasted, subdued, wild—take your choice. There's a new seat to fit every personality and—the best part—all will fit your toilet. Just a matter of unscrewing two nuts at the base of the seat to remove the old and put on the new. The seat-lid combination comes with its own hinge and nuts.

Note: Should you move into an old house and, when you first remove the toilet tank lid, find the inner workings a real shambles, flee to the nearest friendly hardware store and ask for a toilet tank repair kit. The price is reasonable and the kit will have all parts necessary to rejuvenate that ailing necessity.

You now know everything there is to know about the inner secrets of a toilet tank. May your days and nights be free of running toilets. Happy flushing!

11

Plumbing Nuisances—Their Diagnosis and Cure

The Waste Disposer Gives You the Silent Treatment

There are only two things you can do with this whirling dervish:

1. Avoid trying to make it chew up paper, string, silverware, and diamond rings.
2. The following, when you've fed it things you shouldn't have.

Turn on the switch *momentarily* and listen carefully. Do you hear a hum? Is the motor straining to turn but can't?

If so, probably something is wedged against one of the cutting edges (the bumps on opposite sides of the bottom rotor plate). With the switch and water *off,* remove all loose trash from inside the unit. Then, brace your thumb and fingers against the bumps holding the cutting edges and try to turn the rotor counterclockwise. If possible, turn it through several revolutions counterclockwise and then clockwise. Remove your hand and turn on the switch. There's a good chance it'll work perfectly.

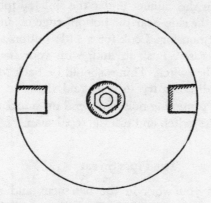

CUTTING EDGES ON
DISPOSER ROTOR PLATE —
LOOKING DOWN INTO
DISPOSER.

If, when you originally turned on the switch momentarily, you did *not* hear a hum, with the switch off, clean out the disposer as above. Then, look for an "overload switch" on the

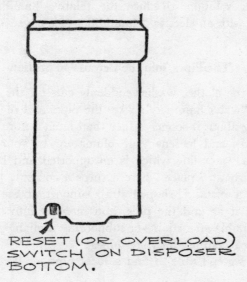

RESET (OR OVERLOAD)
SWITCH ON DISPOSER
BOTTOM.

motor housing (in the cabinet under the sink). Probably the switch will be on the side near the bottom edge or on the bottom of the motor housing. Look for a little button about the size of a pencil eraser. Push it, and, with your hand safely outside, turn on the switch. Things should be back to normal. *But,* should the disposer try to start and then cut itself off again, make loud protesting noises, or send up smoke signals— quickly turn off the switch and call the repairman.

The Pipes Sweat

In summer when you work in the basement and raindrops keep falling on your head and the floor (in a straight line!), it's because the humidity is high, the water in the pipe running along the ceiling is cold, and someone is or has been using the water, probably to water the lawn. There's a quick and easy cure: Go to the hardware store and buy foam insulation formed precisely to fit around the pipe. Keep it in place with cloth tape along the seam.

Another solution: Reduce the relative humidity in the basement with an electric dehumidifier (see page 210).

The Pipes Join the Percussion Section

If, when the clothes washer suddenly cuts off the water, the resulting "water hammer" shakes the pipes and the house, do something about it sooner rather than later, before it tightens your nerves and loosens your plumbing. In your basement look for a water line which is unsupported and hangs loose (particularly at a place where it turns a corner). If you find one, buy a metal U-shaped strap support at the hardware store, put it around the pipe, and screw it into the nearest wood available (floor joists or subflooring probably). Hanging loose is great, but not for water pipes!

If you weren't able to find a loose pipe, or if the support

that you put in didn't help much, ask your plumber to check your water pressure. Depending upon the location of your house, it may be much too high and it may be necessary to install a pressure reducing valve. On the other hand, the solution may be a simple air surge chamber, which is nothing more than a vertical piece of capped pipe with air trapped in it installed in the water line near the clothes washer. The trapped air acts as a cushion to absorb the force of the flowing water when it suddenly stopped.

Water pressure that is too high is good *only* when you are watering the lawn. In addition to producing "water hammer" it's a prime cause of rapid washer failure in faucets.

A Faucet Squirts or Drizzles Instead of Gushing

If your faucet is typical of those manufactured since 1955, it is equipped with a cylindrical gadget called an aerator threaded onto the end of the spout. Its function is to minimize splashing by forcing air to mix with the flowing water. Unfortunately, tiny pieces of sand and other matter carried by the water get trapped in the aerator and begin to reduce the flow. Because the aerator works by forcing the water through very fine holes, three or four specks of sand are enough to reduce water flow by 30% or more. So, if you have the feeling that once upon a time your faucet delivered more water in a more even stream than it does now, the time has arrived to clean the aerator.

PLASTIC RIM WITH
COPPER SCREEN
CENTER

PERFORATED
METAL FLANGE

COPPER METAL
SCREEN WITH
COPPER RIM.

Using your hands, turn the aerator *clockwise* (when looking from above) to loosen it. If it doesn't budge, dry it, wrap it with a layer of adhesive tape, and try again. If it still refuses to turn, wrap it with another layer of tape (to protect the chrome finish) and use pliers. When it does come off, you'll find a rubber or composition washer, a brass or plastic plate with small holes, and one or more brass screens. Clean each part with an old toothbrush and abrasive cleaner, then reassemble the pieces as you found them.

If the screen is missing, the washer is rotten, and things are generally in foul shape, replace the whole aerator; it's inexpensive.

The Kitchen Sink Sprayer Fizzles

A sprayer works by diverting almost all the water from the spout to the hose and spray nozzle. At least, that's the way it's supposed to work. When it doesn't, the hose is kinked, the nozzle stopped up, or that ingenious little device called a "diverter valve" is on the blink.

First, check out the hose. It hangs under the sink in an arc suspended between the connection under the faucet and the nozzle. Old hoses can develop a crease at the bend that cuts off the water or reduces its flow to the point the diverter valve can't operate; or, the hose can just be badly twisted. If there's a crease, straighten the hose and try wrapping with black, plastic electrical tape. Overlap the tape about 1/4". If there's a leak at the crease, replace the whole spray unit.

Next, the nozzle. Using your hand, unscrew (counterclockwise) and remove the unit on the end of the nozzle. It may be a round, ridged plastic piece or a chrome aerator (see page 113). If necessary, use pliers but grip gently if it's plastic and wrap twice with tape if it's chrome. In any case, clean and replace the unit. Now, how's it working?

Any trouble remaining points squarely at the diverter valve.

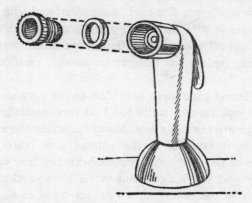

This little gizmo sits free right in the joint where the big spout swivels. Unscrew the knurled ring that holds the spout, lift off the spout, and there it is.

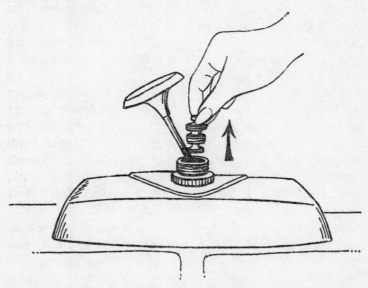

Grasp the little metal stem with the flattened end and lift the diverter valve out (it may have fallen out when you lifted off the spout). Clean it and feel around in the seat where it fits to see if there is any grit that could have interfered with its operation. Replace it *with the stem up* and then replace the spout. Open the cut-off valve and try the spray nozzle again. If it still won't work, replace the diverter valve with an identical new one.

If you found your spray hose shot or the nozzle cracked or defective, replacement units for both are available—fittings on all sinks are the same size. Simply unscrew the end of the hose where it attaches to the control unit (directly *under* the center of the unit) and replace with the new one. I said "simply"—and that's right. But you'll have to clean out the cabinet under the sink so that you can crawl in to reach the connection! And don't forget the cut-off valve!

12

Plumbing Emergencies and How to Meet Them Gracefully

FLOOD!

If that awful day ever arrives when you find the basement afloat, go ahead and panic—but only for a moment. There's no use adding tears to the flood. If your basement is equipped with a sump pump, it should be pumping furiously and, if it's not clogged, removing the water as fast as it gets to the pump. In addition to those initiated by heavy rain or melting snow, floods in otherwise dry basements have four chief sources: a rusted-out water heater tank, a burst clothes washer hose, a burst water pipe, and, in some houses, a malfunctioning sump pump.

Your first action must be to stop the flow of water. Of course, if you've had a week of rain, and water is pouring through a crack in the wall, there's not a lot you can do; but if the flood has been inspired by a leaky tank, hose, or pipe, your first move should be to turn off the main water supply valve.

Your next thought must be for your safety: IF YOU BECOME ANY PART OF AN ELECTRICAL SHORT CIRCUIT WITH YOUR FEET IN WATER, ELECTROCUTION IS ALMOST CERTAIN. DON'T pick up any electrical appliance out of the water while it is still plugged in. In fact, even pulling the plug, if the plug is at all defective, can be disastrous. If you're at all uncertain about the condition of a plug, wear a dry glove or wrap the plug in a dry cloth before pulling it.

Now that you have your valuables to high ground, the flow stanched, and the wet appliances unplugged, how do you get rid of the water? In the absence of a working sump pump, you dip and mop and squeeze and dip and mop and squeeze —unless you have had the forethought to read the next few sentences *before* the catastrophe. In that case, you will have been to the hardware store to buy one of two dandy little devices for such a time as this. The first is a remarkably simple little brass or plastic water pump that attaches to the cold water faucet in the laundry tub and requires no electricity. When the faucet is turned on, it pumps water through a hose directly from the floor into the tub drain. It's not the fastest pump in the world, but it certainly beats mops and sponges alone.

The second gadget for such an occasion is an inexpensive water pump which attaches directly to the chuck of your ¼" electric drill. BUT, because of the danger of electric shock, don't use it unless your drill has a grounded plug (three prongs) *and* the wall outlet is grounded. That is, the wall outlet and plug must either look like this:

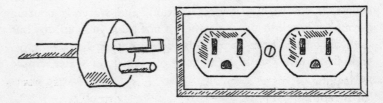

or the little green wire that sticks out of the adapter on the
plug for your drill must be fastened to one of the screws that
hold the outlet fixture in place:

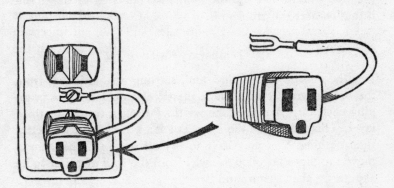

With the flood under control, you're ready to locate the
cause, simply by opening the main water valve and watching.
If you discover the need for a new washer hose, it's wise to
replace both hot and cold hoses at the same time, even though
only one gave way; it's also wise to buy high-quality replacements. If the water gushes out from the water heater, you're
in for a significant investment. You should choose your new
water heater knowing that although the purchase cost of an
electric water heater is quite low, its operating cost is quite
high, and its life expectancy is relatively low. Your choice of a
replacement heater may depend, therefore, on the length of
time you expect to own your home.

If the leak came from a break in a water pipe, the next section should be helpful.

A PIPE SPRINGS A LEAK

A leaking pipe and a leaking faucet (see page 96) are horses
of two different colors. A leaking pipe is big trouble.

Drainpipes or pipes carrying water under pressure can be patched temporarily or permanently, and a temporary patch can be a lifesaver—or at least a housesaver. But *first* cut off the water and don't use the appliance attached to the drain, if that's where the problem is.

Temporary Patch

Dry the outside of the pipe, and, starting several inches from the break, wrap it with black plastic electrical tape, overlapping each turn half the tape width. Put on a second or third layer. This won't last too long, but it's a heck of a lot better than nothing. You may have to pry off some straphangers to move the pipes far enough away from the wall or rafter to be able to get the tape around it.

Permanent Patch

Probably the best and most easily applied patch is that universal cure-all—epoxy. Remove all grease and dirt with a simple abrasive cleaner and then steel wool. Rinse the surface of the pipe and dry it thoroughly. Then apply the epoxy (liquid or putty type) liberally over and around the break, following directions from the package. Let it cure overnight before turning on the water again. Special epoxy patch kits for leaking pipes are available in hardware stores.

A DRAIN STOPS DRAINING

Your First Move

Lavatory, sink and tub: Take a look at the drain plug, if there is one. Ten to one it's removable simply by lifting or by twisting in one direction or the other while lifting, or by unscrewing counterclockwise. Use your hands and don't be afraid to get rough with it. If it's the pull-out type and you had to work pretty hard to get it out, probably it was bound by hair around the bottom. Once it's out, remove the debris and clean the plug with an abrasive cleaner. Before you put it back, turn on the water; and if it drains freely, you have it made. If not, or if it's the kitchen sink or laundry tub, try "the gentle approach."

The Gentle Approach

The force cup is much better known as the "plunger" or the "plumber's friend" and it can be yours too. Although nothing but a rubber hemisphere on the end of a wooden stick, it can exert a whopping force—pull as well as push—on a water-filled, plugged drain. Wad wet cloth and stuff it into the overflow holes directly above the main drain (or sometimes under the lip inside the front of the bowl) to make a seal.

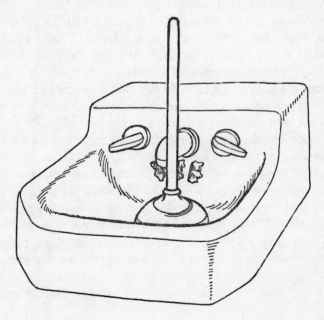

With some water in the bowl (and the drain plug out, if possible)[1] completely cover the main drain hole with the rubber hemisphere of the force cup and plunge the handle straight down and then pull it straight up. The suction resulting from the upward pull is frequently more effective than the plunging action. Don't be surprised if all sort of mess is pulled up into the bowl in the process. This is a good sign that you are getting somewhere. Keep going for a minute or so. If the position of the drain hole or the shape of the bowl make it difficult to seat the rubber hemisphere, a coat of Vaseline on the bottom edge of the latter may help. When you remove the plunger and the water rushes out of the bowl, *you've won*.

On the other hand, if the water doesn't rush out, you're not licked yet. Far from it. Approach ⚡2 is "the trap trick."

The Trap Trick

That chrome plated, U-shaped pipe under the lavatory holds a little water at the bottom of the bend which keeps sewer odors where they belong—not in the house. It also catches diamond rings, bobby pins, and other goodies—as well as Q-Tips, pieces of cotton, and bunches of hair, all of which add up to a plug in the trap. In the unlikely event that plunging hasn't done the trick, one absolutely sure cure is to remove the trap and clean it. And it's no big deal, either.

It's possible, though not probable, that there will be a large square plug at the very bottom of the U-bend. If so, wrap it with tape (masking, adhesive, or plastic) to prevent scratches in the chrome plate, put a container underneath to catch the water, and remove the plug by turning it counterclockwise (when viewed from beneath) with your crescent or monkey

---

[1] Most lavatory drain plugs can be removed by twisting them (by hand) approximately 90° in one direction or the other (usually counterclockwise).

wrench. (Both these wrenches have jaws with flat faces. *Don't* use a wrench with grooves in the faces.) With your finger, you should be able to feel anything causing a stoppage. Fish it out, replace the plug, and check it for a leak. Retighten if necessary, and remove the tape.

Unfortunately, most traps don't have a plug, but the whole trap can be removed easily. On either side of the U-bend you will see hexagonal chrome rings which unscrew to release the trap. Again, with the water catcher in place and the hexagonal rings wrapped with tape, unscrew them (see drawing) all the way and pull down on the trap to remove it. Clean it out thoroughly (an abrasive cleaner and an old toothbrush are ideal), check the rubber gasket in each ring and replace the trap. If the gasket is beat up, take the trap to the hardware store and replace both gaskets. Usually the hexagonal rings don't have to be extremely tight to prevent leaks.

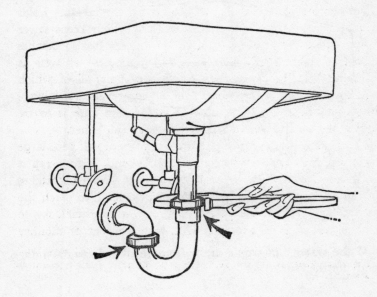

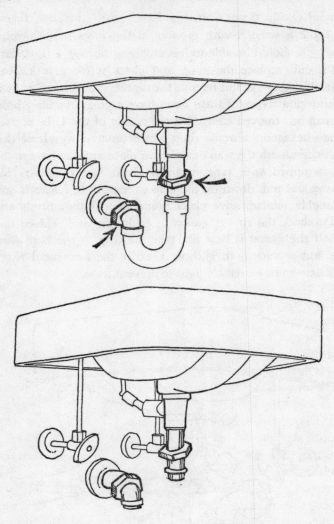

If the water *still* won't drain from the bowl, you're now ready for the "snake act."

The Snake (or Auger)

This is a long, metal coil, somewhat smaller in diameter than your little finger, with a slight bulge in the coil on one end and a movable bent handle on the other. A 10′ snake is about right. Twisting and pushing allows the coil to "snake" its way around pipe bends until you reach and break through the stoppage. If there's a drain plug at the bottom of the U-trap, remove it; otherwise, remove the U-trap itself (see page 122). Push the bulbous end of the snake into the drain pipe *as far as you can make it go,* then loosen the set screw on the bent handle, slide it to within a foot of the pipe opening, and tighten the screw. Now, using both hands, rotate the handle and push.

As the snake goes in, move the handle back—but not more than about a foot at a time. When the snake stops going in, keep twisting and pushing to tear up the obstruction. Don't worry about the scraping noise the snake makes—you won't damage the drain. Keep twisting as you pull the snake out; if the stoppage was within reach, probably you'll see pieces of it on the end. Don't forget to put the trap back on!

If the obstruction couldn't be reached with your 10′ snake, now is the time to call your favorite plumber.

Commercial drain cleaners: There's no lack of liquids or solids sold to help you unstop your drain; they're easy to use and frequently work. *But* they are all either very *basic* (caustic) or very *acidic,* so there's some hazard involved. A splash in the eye could do irreparable damage. And they won't do one thing more than the techniques we've already covered. Once a cleaner is put into the drain, if the stoppage is not relieved, then what? You (or the plumber) fall back on the methods above—but this time you are working with a drain pipe full of caustic or acid. My advice: Stick to the mechanical methods if the drain is completely stopped.

A TOILET CLOGS

At the hardware store there's a plunger available made especially to fit the hole in the toilet bowl. If your toilet is stopped up, definitely buy this plumber's toilet friend (or should I say toilet plumber's friend?). There's a great chance that's all you'll need.

However, if things are so fouled up that stronger measures are needed, drag out the snake.

If the bowl is full, use something to scoop out as much water as possible. Then, grab the snake about two feet from bulbous end and push it into the big hole facing you at the base of the bowl. It will go up and over the back of the hole, down the opening under the bowl, and into the drain pipe. Twist and push and push and twist until you've hit and cleared the obstruction—or you've run out of snake. When the blockage is cleared, you'll notice a definite bubbling or change of level in the bowl. Don't flush the toilet yet! Add water from a pan or bucket to the bowl. If the line is open, you won't be able to fill the bowl because it will overflow (down the drain this time!), just as it does in the normal flushing action. If the bowl fills up to the rim bulge, the line's not open and if you've used the full length of snake—again it's time to yell for your plumber.

13

Basic Procedures

So This Is the First Time You've Swung a Hammer?

Nails are a lot easier to drive than cars, but driving or removing a nail correctly does take practice. Not much, but practice. You'll need to master both of these skills and in the process get rid of any fears about tackling jobs which, at first, may seem too complex. Remember, there's nothing in this book *you* can't do.

Buy, find, borrow, or purloin the following necessities (see list page 23 ff):
1. A hammer.
2. A couple of dozen 4d ("4 penny") common nails and the same number of 4d finishing nails.
3. A nail set.
4. A scrap piece of 2″×4″ lumber, 3′ long, or longer, for practice.

Find a clear, flat place (workbench top, floor, driveway) and put the 2″×4″ down on its wide side. (If you're working on the floor or driveway, you'll certainly have to kneel.) But before attempting to drive a nail, get the feel of the hammer. Firmly grasp the handle (as you would shake hands or hold a tennis racket) in the middle and swing the hammer a number of times through a small arc until the sensation seems much less strange and awkward. Use your arm, not just your wrist. Hold the wood firmly with one hand and starting with the hammer head flat on the wood and holding the handle parallel with the surface, raise the hammer and hit the 2"×4". At the moment the head hits the wood, the face and handle of the hammer must again be parallel with the surface. Don't worry about denting the wood. Actually, the indentations are quite revealing: they should be symmetrical; if the mark made by the head is deeper on one side than another, the hammer was tilted in that direction when it should have been flat against the wood. Practice until you're satisfied.

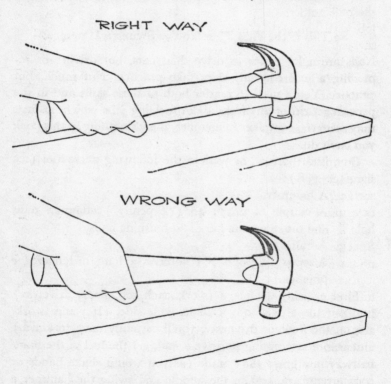

RIGHT WAY

WRONG WAY

Next, move your grip on the handle to a point about three-fourths of the way to the end. There's a new feel when you swing the hammer now; get used to it. Then hammer the board some more until the motion and correct positioning of your arm and the hammer become more natural.

At last! A nail! Between your thumb and first two fingers hold a 4d common nail perpendicular in the middle of the 2″×4″. Keep your fingers at least halfway up the nail.[1] Grip the hammer in the halfway position and tap the nail lightly— but squarely in the middle of the hammer face—once or twice to start it into the wood. Remove your fingers and, with the nail standing alone, tap it once or twice more. Move your hand to the three-fourths position on the handle and drive the nail until the head is very close to the surface. Finish the job with lighter blows until the nail head is flush with the surface.

If the nail entered the wood at an angle instead of perpendicularly, the hammer head either wasn't exactly on target or the face and handle weren't parallel with the board at impact. It's perfectly legitimate to straighten the nail with your fingers between blows. Continue driving 4d common nails until you have amassed a record of five consecutive perfect ones.

Complete this session using finishing nails. This type is designed to be driven until its small head is close to the wood surface; it is then driven approximately ⅛″ *below* the surface, using a pointed tool known as a "nail set." The small hole in the wood left above the nail head can be filled with Spackle or wood putty (see page 156) and painted, leaving no trace of its presence.

Exactly as with the common nails, drive 4d finishing nails until each head protrudes just above the wood. Then, grasping the nail set firmly between the thumb and first two fingers and, holding it perpendicular, press the point into the small indentation of the nail head. Holding the hammer in the halfway position, tap the nail set until the head of the nail is countersunk approximately ⅛″. Should the nail set jump off

[1] To minimize your discomfort in case you strike finger instead of nail.

the head and dent the wood, hold it more firmly against the nail. Again, don't stop until you have a score of five perfect ones.

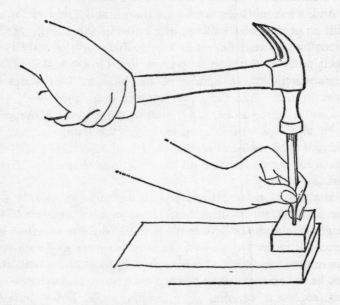

But what about nails you want to *remove,* not drive? They are easy to pull provided the head is sticking out of the wood as much as ⅛″ to ¼″. The "claw" of the hammer is made just for this purpose.

Drive several nails (common or finishing types), leaving a portion of each protruding from the 2″×4″. Here's how to remove them:

Place the points of the claw on either side of the nail, and, with some force, slide the claw forward so that the nail wedges in the narrowing gap between the jaws. Then, with your hand gripping the end of the handle, rock the hammer back. Considerable leverage and force are required if the nail is deeply embedded—which is why your grip must be near the end of the handle.

Should you want to remove a nail from a wall (or from anything you wish to avoid scarring), first place a thin piece of wood or heavy cardboard under the hammer head.

And what about a nail completely embedded in wood with no portion of it sticking out? You're licked; forget about removing it. But you can fill the hole above it with Spackle or wood putty (see page 156) so no one will know it is there. If necessary, set the nail before spackling (see page 129).

Making Shorter Boards Out of Longer Ones

Using a square or combination square, draw a perpendicular pencil line across the 2″×4″ at some point 2″ or 3″ from one end. To draw this line, place the edge of the handle of the square snugly against the side of the board. This assures that the metal blade of the square is perpendicular to the board length. Holding the square firmly against the wood, run the pencil along the blade across the board. (Watch out for nails! There may be some if the board has been used before. Nails *can* be cut, but not by a crosscut saw. This is the hacksaw's job [see page 133].) A 2″×4″ makes just a fine practice board for sawing, but, in contrast to nailing, it would be somewhat more than difficult to cut it when it's flat on the floor. If you don't own sawhorses (see page 132), a workbench or sturdy wooden box or old chair makes a suitable platform.

Find something that suits and put the 2″×4″ on it, wide dimension down, so that the pencil mark is several inches beyond the edge of the support. Stand facing the side of the 2″×4″ with one hand pressing down on it to keep it in place. Grip the handle of the crosscut saw, and with the blade perpendicular and making an angle of approximately 45° with the board, place the toothed edge of the saw *near* the saw handle on the far end of the pencil line at the board's edge. Now, slowly draw the saw toward you. Pick up the blade and

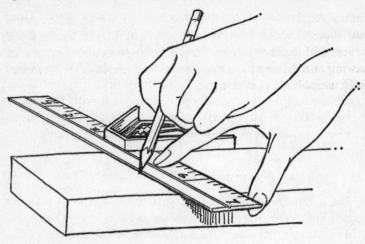

repeat in exactly the same place on the board. The preliminary cut you just made will act as a guide for subsequent full strokes. Continue, alternately pulling and pushing the saw while putting moderate pressure on it. If the saw tilts from perpendicular or turns to the right or left, the cut will stray from the pencil line. When you near the end of the job, continue sawing but ease the pressure on the blade to avoid splitting the wood on the last few strokes. If the piece of wood being cut off is longer than a foot or two, someone holding that end is a big help.

Cut off several 3″ or 4″ sections of the 2″×4″ until you have the knack.

A Brace of Useful Horses

Two sawhorses provide the classic support for things being sawed, painted, or sanded, as well as for countless other jobs. They can be bought, but why not make them?

The hardware store sells kits containing the four metal

braces required (and simple directions); all you need do is
saw some 2″×4″s the proper lengths and attach them to the
braces with nails or screws. In the process you gain practice in
sawing and driving nails (or screws) and produce two wonderfully useful holders of things.

Cut That Nail

The hacksaw's made to do just that. Its teeth are set in one
direction (pointing forward away from the handle) so that
cutting is done *only* on the push stroke.

Let's try it. Drive a nail about three-fourths of its length
into the 2″×4″. Then clamp the wood in a vise (or have
someone hold it securely on suitable support) so that the nail
is horizontal and in the clear. Grip the handle of the hacksaw with one hand; put the other on the front of the hacksaw
top brace. With the saw perpendicular to the nail, place the
rear part of the blade (near the handle) on the nail and, with
moderate pressure, pull the saw to you. Repeat this operation
two or three times to make a shallow groove in the nail which
keeps the blade from slipping sideways when you begin the

forward stroke. Now, place the *front* part of the blade (away from the handle) on the nail and, with moderate pressure, push the saw forward. On the return stroke use less pressure. Again on the forward stroke use moderate pressure with both hands. Keep going and before long you've cut the nail completely through. Smooth the jagged end with a file.

Things That Stick and Fill

Sticky situations aren't all bad; in fact, they can be terrific: adhesives, glues, caulks, and tapes, as a start. And now that they are available in such a bewildering number and variety, how do you know which one to use? Sit back and we'll make some sense out of the situation; then, make your choice, follow the manufacturer's directions, and you will be struck —and stuck—with the great results.

Crack and joint fillers: Caulks are somewhat elastic, weather-resistant fillers which stick well to a variety of surfaces. Their chief use is to fill primarily, but not exclusively, exterior cracks and joints, to keep out all sorts of things (bugs, cold air, moisture, dust) and to keep heat in. Until recently, available caulking materials tended to become dry, brittle, and to crack and lose their adhesive characteristics rather quickly. The newer ones adhere tighter, much longer, and won't dry, shrink or pull away from the crack they are filling. Most can be painted.

Caulk comes in tubes from which you can squeeze it like toothpaste or in disposable cartridges which fit into a simple "caulk gun." Both are easy and fun to use. Directions are on the tube. Just be sure the crack or joint is clean and old caulk or loose paint has been removed. If the crack is deeper than ½" or is wider than your little finger, partially fill it by tamping in oakum, a rope-like filler made specifically for this purpose. You can get it at the hardware store where you bought the caulk. As you squeeze and move the "gun" or tube along in firm contact with the crack, it will lay down a "bead" of caulk which is convex. Resist the temptation to smooth it with your finger; leave it just as it is.

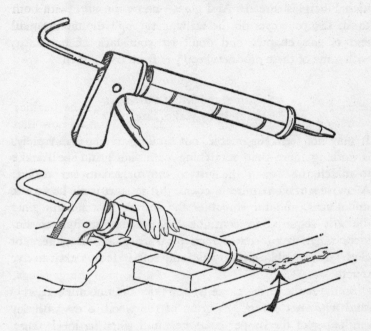

Where are you going to use this caulk? Any exterior joint or crack: around window frames, door frames, door sills, where brick meets wood, corner joints, cracks in mortar. What kind of house needs caulking? Every one that has ever been built. There is nothing wrong in using caulk on the interior in situations similar to those on the exterior. However, cracks in walls and woodwork are best filled another way (see chapter 15).

Tapes and glues: When you see "tape" do you think "Scotch"? Certainly it was the granddaddy of modern transparent self-stick tapes, and now, in addition, comes in "double stick" and "magic transparent" variations. All are much imitated. A variety of extremely useful tapes are available for just about any job you can imagine, from the common "brown paper" tape that you wet to self-stick tape reinforced with Fiberglas threads. And glues—name the job, there's one to fit. Let your eyes do the walking through the tables at the end of this chapter and don't let your lack of familiarity with some of these products keep you from trying them.

Sanding, the Great Paradox:
Scratching Makes Smooth

It may not seem reasonable, but sanding to smooth or polish is nothing more than scratching with fine grit. The trick is to match the size of the grit to the surface to be tackled: A coarse surface requires a coarse grit to start it on its way to smoothness, and the smoother the surface becomes the finer the grit required to continue the process. Sandpaper surfaces range from coarse rock particles glued to paper (or cloth) to invisible grit so fine and soft it feels satiny to the touch.

So the name of the game is: the finer the smoother. Always sand *with,* not *across,* the grain of the wood. Start with the sandpaper of the proper coarseness and when its job is done, change to the next finer grade; continue using finer grades of grit until you have the surface you want.

Short cuts? Only one. You can get away with using every other decreasing grit size, but it's probably better not to skip any.

But, what is the proper starting grade (coarseness) of sandpaper? Since it's unlikely that you would be using crude, rough lumber, let's assume that you're going to sand a piece of "dressed" lumber bought at the lumberyard or a piece of furniture to be refinished. Start with ⋕2–0 (medium coarseness) then go to a ⋕3–0 (fine), a ⋕4–0 (fine), and finally to ⚹5–0 (fine). Stop sanding in between ⚹2–0 and ⚹5–0 if the surface fits your requirements. Probably ⚹3–0 will be sufficient if the wood is to be painted. If it is to be varnished, go all the way to ⚹5–0, or even ⚹6–0.

Between coats of paint or varnish, hand sanding with ⚹6–0 (or finer) will work wonders.

The Finish You Love to Touch

If it's that velvet-soft, hand-rubbed finish you are after, the final touch must be done by hand *after* the ⚹5–0 or ⚹6–0 treatment of a varnished piece.

Buy some rottenstone (great name, no? Sometimes called "tripoli"), available at paint and hardware stores, and make a thick slurry with either water or oil (common cooking oil or lubricating oil is fine). Coat a pad of folded cloth with the mixture and rub the finish evenly using moderate pressure. Check your progress frequently by cleaning and examining the finish. It takes energy and time, but the result is something to see.

Silver

What's silver doing here? No, I'm not going to tell you to polish your silver with sandpaper. But you must admit I was talking about polishing, even though it was the finish on a piece of wood. There are ways and there are ways to polish silver. Here are the best—some old, some new, all borrowed—all for you.

Silver cleaning techniques that don't polish: Heavily tarnished silver is best cleaned *first* and *then* polished. Cleaning will remove the difficult to reach tarnish on ornate silver as well as tarnish on pieces that have been neglected and have become pitted, and this is more common than you might like to think. No cleaning or polishing will remove deep pits—just the tarnish in the pits. But that does wonders for appearance.

The old aluminum foil trick: Cover the bottom of an enameled or glass cooking pan with aluminum foil and add one (1) teaspoon of baking soda, one-half (½) teaspoon of salt, and about two (2) quarts of hot water from the faucet. Heat the water to the boiling point, turn off the heat, and submerge the pieces of silver, making certain that each piece touches the aluminum foil or touches another piece of silver which is touching the foil. That's all. Watch the tarnish begin to disappear! After five minutes, rinse and polish (see below). That odor is from the sulfur which caused the tarnish in the first place!

I didn't say use an aluminum pan. Why? Although the cleaning would be just fine, your aluminum pan would be tarnished. Notice the appearance of the aluminum foil when you remove it.

Dip-type cleaners: These are great and are available in housewares departments. They do aluminum's job much more rapidly but cost considerably more than a teaspoon of baking soda and a piece of foil. However, a dip cleaner may be used again and again. For silver pieces too large to dip, wet a piece of cloth with the solution and apply it to the silver; rinse the silver and your hands afterward. The odor developed by the dip is the same as that from the aluminum foil method.

Polishes: Old-fashioned paste polishes are still very much on the market for one very good reason—they work. Use as a pad a small piece of soft cloth folded several times. Purists won't use anything but the polish and fingers. However, on ornate silver an old, soft toothbrush plus polish works wonders. All the black that develops as you polish silver is super-fine particles of metallic silver. Don't worry about it; you aren't damaging your silver—and you won't with any of these methods.

Tarnish preventive polishes: These latest developments in the evolution of silver polishes live up to their claim. They coat the silver with an unbelievedly thin protective film that is colorless, odorless, tasteless, and harmless—but keep out the sulphur contaminants in the air (from burning gas or fuel oil) which cause tarnish. Follow the simple directions and your polishing jobs will be fewer and further between.

Brass and copper too: Brass or copper is also best tackled in two steps: Clean it first with a "copper cleaner" (grocery store) and then use a copper and brass tarnish preventive polish, or, to cut down on your inventory of cleaners, simply use the tarnish preventive polish made for silver. It works equally well for brass and copper.

Note: Some brass or copper pieces are lacquered to prevent tarnish. If the lacquer film has deteriorated and the piece has begun to tarnish, the only cure is to remove the coating (conventional paint removers will do the job) and then polish as above.

Some No-No's: Don't leave silver in contact with any of the following materials longer than the time required for a meal: Egg, mustard, mayonnaise, sauerkraut, or salt. On standing, all of these will attack silver.

ADHESIVES and GLUES

NAME	USES AND CHARACTERISTICS
Cellulose Glue	China, wood, metal, glass, paper, leather; waterproof, somewhat flexible.
Contact Adhesives	Metals, ceramics, wood, leather, tile, rubber; water resistant.

NAME	USES AND CHARACTERISTICS
Epoxy Glue	All-purpose; for use on metal, glass, wood, rubber, brick, concrete, ceramics, Fiberglas. Waterproof; makes extremely strong bond.
Filler Glues	All metals. Not affected by water, oil, or gasoline.
Hot Glues	Wood, pottery, leather, fabrics; flexible. Applied by an electric heating "gun."
Iron Cement	Stops leaks in water and steam pipes; use on metals, wood, masonry. Expands as sets.
Plastic Glues	Vinyl plastic. Waterproof, flexible.
Resin Glues	Primarily for use on wood. Waterproof; not affected by boiling water, acids, alkalies, solvents. Primarily for use on interior wood. Water resistant.
Spray Adhesives	Paper, glass, metal, cork, rubber, pads, mats, floor covering, gaskets.
Stick Glues	Paper, fabrics, photos, Styrofoam. Not waterproof or heatproof.
Tile Cement and Grout	Not affected by water, steam, oil, soap, heat.
White Glues	Porous materials (wood, paper, cloth, pottery, Styrofoam). Not for use on photos or metal. Not waterproof or heatproof.

CAULKS, SEALANTS, AND FILLERS

NAME	USES AND CHARACTERISTICS
General Purpose Exterior Caulks	For sealing exterior cracks and joints.
Special Purpose Sealers for Reefing Gutters, Cement Cracks, and Asphalt Cracks; Tub Caulks	As indicated by name.
Fillers Patching Plaster and Spackle	For use on interior plaster and wallboard.

TAPES

NAME	USES AND CHARACTERISTICS
Aluminum Foil Tape	General indoor and outdoor use. Watertight; paintable.
Duct Tape	See Aluminum Foil Tape
Fiberglas Reinforced Tape	Sticks to most surfaces; moisture-proof; extremely strong.
Friction Tape	Old-fashioned electrical tape; largely supplanted by Plastic Electrical Tape.
Double-Faced Tape	Used to anchor rugs, indoor and outdoor carpeting and linoleum. A double-faced masking tape.
Gummed Paper Tape	Old stand-by. Requires moistening; for use on paper products.

NAME	USES AND CHARACTERISTICS
Heat-Sensitive Tape	Used to repair cloth; washable.
Masking Tape	Inexpensive, for temporary use; chiefly used for masking during painting.
Cloth Tape	General use. Repairs tears, reinforces; also used to tape heating ducts. Waterproof, strong; comes in variety of widths and colors.
Pipe Joint Tape	Made of Teflon. Used to seal pipe threads; withstands extreme pressure and heat and cold.
Plastic Electrical Tape	For electrical repairs; good adhesion, somewhat elastic, waterproof.
Strapping Tape	For wrapping packages. Nonsticking, comes with necessary metal or plastic locks. Removable and reusable.
Transparent Tape	The ubiquitous "Scotch tape," which has many imitators.
Weatherstrip Tape	Repairs leaks in water hoses, plastic pools; used on tool handles. Withstands heat and cold, indoors and outdoors.

14

Ye Olde X-Ray Eye

WHAT'S BEHIND THAT WALL

The last chapter was about basic procedures, but there is one procedure that is so basic that I'm going to give it a whole little chapter of its own. I'm talking about how you find out how a certain wall in your home is constructed. You've got to know about a wall's construction before you can do anything much to it—hanging heavy pictures on it, for example, or building shelves.

WALL CONSTRUCTION

Let's take a look at some cross-sections showing typical wall constructions; yours will be one of these:

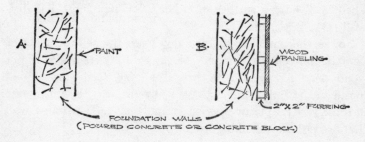

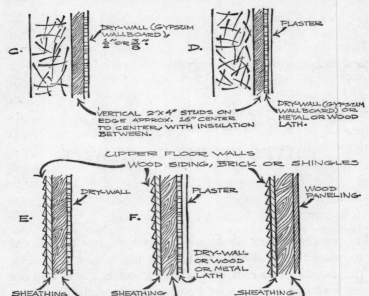

Basement

Let's talk about A. Ten to one if your basement isn't "finished" you'll see the relatively rough, painted surface of poured concrete or the outline of concrete blocks. A dead giveaway that your wall is Type A.

However, that portion of your basement which is "finished" will have a surface of either wood paneling (B), dry-wall (C), or plaster (D).

So, in the basement, if you don't see the telltale signs of poured concrete or concrete block, or if the surface is not wood paneling, then it is typical 2"×4" stud construction found in the upper floors. A stud, by the way, is simply one of those vertical pieces of wood (usually 2"×4") within a wall that holds the whole thing up.

First and Second Floors

From the studs inward, C is identical with E, and D is identical with F, and this is the portion of interest here.

Wood paneling in the upper floors generally isn't put on $2'' \times 2''$ (or $1'' \times 2''$) furring strips as it is in the basement; it's nailed directly over the $2'' \times 4''$ studs (if put up at the time of construction) or it's simply stuck with adhesives to the walls (if done after construction of the walls).

Boring holes in A, which requires drilling through concrete or cinder block masonry can be a tough job; information about equipment and procedure appears in chapters 15 and 16. In contrast, the trickiest thing about boring holes through plaster or wood surfaces is deciding where to drill the hole. Some situations require that you drill *into* a stud; others require that you drill *between* the studs. Thus, the prime question is, "Where, oh, where is that little wood stud?"

LOCATING STUDS

Those $2'' \times 4''$ studs hiding in walls aren't exactly a cinch to locate—unless you know how. And locate them you must before starting to hang anything from an expansion or toggle bolt fastener, or even from a nail. (With the fasteners, you've got to avoid the studs, but with a nail, you aim for one.)

If your wall is dry-wall construction (gypsum wallboard nailed over studs) and *if* the builders were so sloppy that indentations are visible in a vertical line where the wallboard was nailed, these indentations pinpoint the studs. Glance along the surface with your eye a few inches away from the wall and facing a source of light; the indentations should stand out like sore thumbs.

But suppose there aren't any indentations? In that case

either your dry-wall man was very careful or your wall is plaster, and you will need a stud finder. There are two types available: one whose operation depends upon the location of a nail by a tiny magnet; the other (sometimes called a "wall dowser") on the difference of resiliency of the wall at and away from a stud. Both are inexpensive, readily available, and easy to use following the directions supplied with them.

But there is a still cheaper stud finder. In fact, it's free. With a little practice, faith, silence, and a good ear, you can locate a stud by moving horizontally along the wall while tapping with the second joint of your first finger.[1] As you near the stud, the wall sound will gradually increase in pitch to a maximum over the stud. Ye of little faith can confirm it by one of the other methods.

Another tip-off to a stud location is one or more nail indentations in the *baseboard* where it was nailed to the stud. If you can't see the nail indentations in the baseboard, the magnetic-type locater might be useful here also.

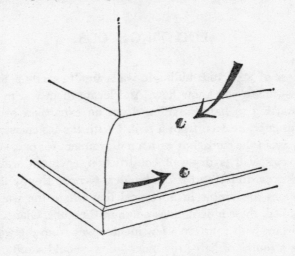

[1] Actually, I prefer the second joint of my *second* finger. *De gustibus . . .*

Still another clue to stud location: the little metal boxes holding light switches and receptacles are always nailed on the side of a stud. Other studs can be located *approximately* by measuring from the one where the switch is attached, or from a corner. Studs are supposed to be 16″ apart, center to center, *but* the distance between them occasionally varies, so simply measuring from one stud to find another can be risky business. You'd better verify the location by one of the other techniques.

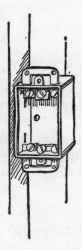

Now that you know what's inside your wall, you're ready to drill a hole in it. Because holes are so important, the next chapter is devoted exclusively to making those you want and filling those you don't.

15

A Whole Chapter on Holes

HOLES YOU WANT

Wherein the mystery surrounding the drilling of a hole is dispelled.

Nails can be hammered directly into wood, but bolts, anchors, Molly bolts, and split-wing fasteners (not to mention screws, which we will talk about later) all require a simple, straight hole.

Drilling a Hole

In wood: The diameter of the hole should be just a trace larger than whatever you are trying to put through it. Select the proper drill bit from your set and place it in the "chuck" of your electric drill and tighten it by rotating the chuck sleeve by hand. Next, insert the chuck key and really tighten; then, remove the chuck key. (Chuck keys are forever getting lost. Using the black electrical variety, tape the two arms of your chuck key securely to the electric cord about 18″ from where it enters the drill. There it is always readily available, easily used, and doesn't interfere with your use of the drill.)

Plug the drill cord into the electric socket and with your right hand around the pistol grip and your left hand holding the body of the drill, slowly squeeze the trigger. Don't jump! If you've followed my advice and bought the continuously variable speed drill, the tighter you squeeze the trigger, the faster the chuck and bit turn. If it's a single speed drill, the bit will be turning perhaps 2,000 to 2,500 rpm. In any event, you'll hear the normal whine of the gears. Try it several times until you get used to holding the drill and are not startled by the sudden whine and power released when you press that trigger. When the drill is working under load (boring a hole) the speed will be somewhat less.

With a pencil, mark the spot on a piece of wood where you want to drill a hole and tap a nail about $\frac{1}{8}''$ to $\frac{1}{16}''$ into this spot to make a starter hole which will keep the drill bit from slipping sideways.

Hold the piece of wood in a vise, use clamps, have someone else hold it down, or in some way firmly secure it. (Never attempt to drill a small piece of unsecured wood—it will spin like a propeller with the bit!) Gripping the drill firmly in both hands, squeeze the trigger and slowly, but with moderate pressure, place the bit against the marked spot, keeping the drill perpendicular to the wood. The bit will move easily through the wood. While it is still running, withdraw the drill and bit. How about that for a neat hole? Two things to watch: Hold the drill firmly and steadily (but not frantically) so that it doesn't wobble as you drill, and make every effort to see that the bit starts out and stays perpendicular to the face of the wood.

Drilling a hole in plaster or gypsum board: Use the same technique for drilling the hole in a plaster or gypsum board wall—after you have located and decided whether you do or don't want to hit a stud and after you've determined that the wall isn't concrete block (see below).

Table

Screw size (flat, round, or oval head)	#2	#3	#4	#5	#6	#7	#8	#9	#10	#12	#14[1]
Bit size for shank hole (inches)		3/32	7/64	1/8	9/64	5/32	11/64	3/16	3/16	7/32	1/4
Bit size for thread hole (inches)		1/16	1/16	5/64	5/64	3/32	7/64	1/8	1/8	9/64	5/32
Screw Lengths:[2] *Shortest available (inches)*	1/4	1/4	3/8	3/8	3/8	3/8	1/2	5/8	5/8	7/8	1
Longest available (inches)	1/2	5/8	3/4	3/4	1 1/2	1 1/2	2	2 1/4	2 1/4	2 1/2	2 3/4

Bit sizes included in a "drill set" (1/16″ to 1/4″ by 64ths):
1/16, 5/64, 3/32, 7/64, 1/8, 9/64, 5/32, 11/64, 3/16, 13/64, 7/32, 15/64, 1/4.

[1] Screw sizes larger than #14 require a bit larger than 1/4″.
[2] Length of flat head screws is measured from top of head to points.
Length of round or oval head screws is measured from bottom of head to point.

Holes for Screws

The hole to make for a screw is a profile of the screw itself. A screw has three parts: the head, the shank, or unthreaded portion, and the shaft, or threaded portion.

Round or oval head screws: First, select the bit just a trace *larger* than the screw shank (hold the bit next to the screw shank and compare) and, after making the starter hole with a nail or awl, drill a hole just *slightly* deeper than the length of the screw shank. Second, select a bit (again by sighting) the same size as the shaft of the screw (the solid portion of the screw surrounded by the threads). Now, in the bottom of the first hole, drill a second hole the length of the screw threads. Practice on a scrap piece of wood and see how elegantly the screw fits. No splitting, no forcing—just right.

You can use the same hole for a flathead screw *if* you use a "finishing washer" under the head.

Flathead screws: Unless they are used with a finishing washer, flathead screws have sharp edges, stick up above the surface of the wood, catch on things, or mar the wood surface if forcibly screwed in without a hole ("countersink") prepared to receive the head.

So—starting with the type hole you drilled for the round or oval head screw, there's only one more step: Using a countersink bit, drill the shallow, tapered hole (countersink) to hold the screw head. Careful, don't go too deep or you'll make the hole larger than the screw head. Practice this operation several times.

You didn't buy a countersink bit? Then select from your set a bit of the same diameter as the screw head and use it. This will work, but takes practice.

If you are planning to use screws, even to a limited extent, go to the hardware store and treat yourself to an "adjustable countersink and screw pilot" which comes in graded sizes, each adjustable to fit three screw sizes. Also available are multibore bits, one for each screw size, which do exactly the same job. Using either of these marvels, in one fell swoop, the hole is made, complete with lead hole, shank hole, and countersink.

Driving the Screw

Choose a screwdriver (square blade or Phillips blade) which fits as exactly as possible the slot in the screw head. A blade too large to seat properly or so small it rattles around in the head slot will so damage the screw head (usually when the screw is not all the way in!) that it is difficult or impossible either to remove it or to complete the job. Another good reason for fitting the driver to the screw: A properly fitting screwdriver is much less likely to jump out of the slot and gouge the wood (or your finger, if you happen to be holding the screw).

Now, with the hole bored, insert the screw and, holding it with one hand and the handle of the screwdriver with the other, place the blade in the head slot and with moderate forward pressure turn about one-half a turn *clockwise*. If the screw does not feel reasonably secure, turn another half turn. Next, no longer holding the screw with your fingers and with moderate pressure against the screw, continue to turn *clockwise* until the base of the screw head is firmly against the wood (if it is a round or oval head) or until the head is flush (level) with the wood surface (if it is a flathead which is being countersunk). Neat job!

If you have trouble with the blade jumping out of the head slot, prepare several holes on a piece of scrap wood and practice driving screws several times. Helps immeasurably.

Drilling a Hole in Masonry

How'd you like to have some shelves attached to that concrete block wall in the basement or the garage? Drilling concrete block calls for really tough "masonry" bits—with carbide tips—and about half the drill speed required for wood. This is no problem for the variable speed drill. Just press the drill and bit against the wall with as much force as you can muster and squeeze the trigger so that the drill runs at about half its full speed. As always, from time to time, check the temperature of the drill housing with your hand. It should be warm; if it is *hot* stop for a while and let the motor cool and then continue. Don't try this job with a hand drill.

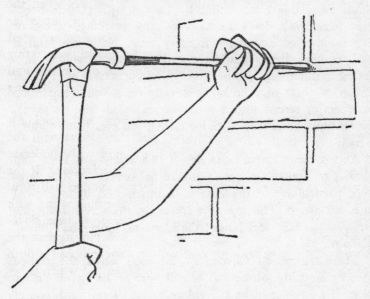

If your budget has kept you drill-less up to this point and you just *have* to put up those shelves (or hang that hose rack), all is not lost—provided you have a strong right arm, a hammer, patience, and a "star" drill. The process is simplicity itself: Hold the point of the star drill firmly perpendicular to the concrete block at the right spot and, with your left hand gripping the drill about one-quarter of the way down from the top, bang away squarely on the drill head while rotating the drill a part of a turn between each blow. The heavier the hammer you can swing, the faster the cutting goes. Protect your hand by wearing a heavy glove and don't hold the drill too close to where the hammer hits.

SCREWS THAT WON'T TIGHTEN

Stash away this rule of thumb: Except with picture hooks (see page 164), don't use nails to hang *anything*. Screws or expansion-type fasteners win every time. Nails are fatal if used to hang things that have moving parts or will be subjected to pulls—up, down, or out. Can openers? Towel racks? Either of these may be hung directly on a wall (expansion fasteners or screws into a stud) or on wood trim (screws). Never nails. Soon they work loose. Did you ever try to tighten a nail?

And it came to pass one day that a screw was loose and instead of tightening, simply turned in its hole. It does happen, particularly in the case of a much-used item screwed into soft wood. The repeated forces on the screw ream the walls of the hole and bingo! the screw no longer has "bite." Then what?

There are options. Check for solid wood behind the reamed hole by inserting a long nail or stiff wire or an awl or an ice pick. If so, you're in luck. Replace the old screw with one of the *same diameter but longer*. It will bite into the new wood and the problem is solved.

If, when you probe the hole for solid wood, there is only "hole," then there are *still* two options: First you can rebuild the hole by partially filling it with wood splinters or match sticks held in place with glue. When the glue is dry, replace the old screw.

Another possibility is to determine the thickness of the

wood by inserting a stiff wire with a right angle bend at the end small enough to go through the hole but large enough to catch on the back side of the wood. Mark the wire at the front surface, remove it, and measure that distance to the end. If the thickness of the wood is not greater than 1″, you can use an expansion fastener. Depending upon the size of the original hole it may be necessary to make it larger to accommodate the fastener.

RICKETY! RICKETY!

Many's the wooden chair with loose legs or back—rickety, crooked, and liable to collapse at exactly the wrong moment, which is anytime. And since the technique for fixing a chair rung that won't stay tight is similar to the technique just described for fixing a screw that won't tighten, I'll digress a minute and tell you what to do about a flimsy chair.

If the piece is so far gone that you can take it apart with a few well-chosen blows of a towel-padded hammer, the job is

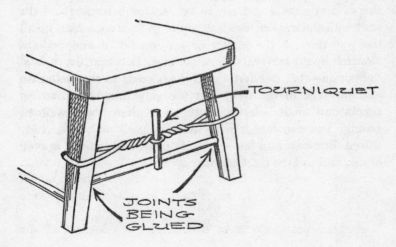

TOURNIQUET

JOINTS BEING GLUED

easy. Remove all the old glue by sanding, apply new glue (see page 139), and reassemble. If, after sanding, you find that the parts fit loosely, coat the rung joint with glue and wrap it with several turns of thread before reinserting it in the hole. Immediately draw all joints tightly together by leading a heavy cord (or small rope) around the outside of adjacent legs (if there are rungs between the legs) and tying the ends together. Then insert a short stick between the two cords and twist it to make a tourniquet. Brace the stick against the rung to keep it from unwinding and to keep the pressure on the joints. It's a good idea to put padding, such as an old towel, under the cord to keep from marring the legs.

HOLES YOU DON'T WANT

Holes and cracks—everybody's house has them. So get the upper hand early in the game.

Holes in plaster and gypsum board: Holes come in all shapes and sizes and have to be tackled accordingly. Let's start with the smaller ones, say, up to $\frac{1}{2}''$ across, which go all the way through the plaster or gypsum board and perhaps were left by the removal of a nail or expansion fastener.

Spackle—that wonderful stuff that's going to save your skin and the hole in the wall. Just the very thing for patching cracks and small holes in plaster or gypsum board walls or ceiling. You can mix it with water yourself or buy it ready mixed. Be smart and buy the ready mixed. It's cheap, smooth as silk, and just the right consistency.

Using your finger (or a screwdriver) fill the back half of the hole with spackling compound and let it dry.

Then overfill the front half of the hole with Spackle, and, holding your 3″ flexible spackling blade at a low angle, draw it with moderate pressure across the hole several times from different directions. Where the hole was, there should be a slight bulge of Spackle while in the surrounding area it should be "feathered" (spread) quite thin.

Let it dry thoroughly[3] and sand lightly with fine sandpaper (※3–0=120 grit).

[3] How long does that take? That's a tough one. Depends on the size and thickness of the patch, the consistency of the patching material, room temperature, and humidity—and whether the patch is on an outside wall. You'll be able to tell when it's dry by the color of the patch and it's temperature. As long as the patch is cooler than the rest of the wall, it's not dry. The time required could vary from fifteen minutes to several hours.

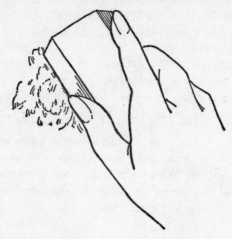

The best way is to wrap the sandpaper around a small block of wood, or, if you have one, a sanding block. Sand until you've just removed the Spackle bulge. Be sure to put a preliminary coat of paint on this area before you paint the rest of the wall.

But suppose you're faced with a hole that goes *all the way through* the wall or ceiling and is too large to patch by the simple method above.

Here's the heart of the problem: There's no back to the hole and you need one to fill against. So—make a back. Any way you can devise is fine. If you're a little low on ingenuity at the moment, others have faced this problem and have come up with some solutions.

Can you see wooden or metal lath through the hole? If so, build layers of Spackle on it.

If there's nothing there, cut a piece of cardboard just narrow enough to go through the hole but several inches longer than the hole's other dimension. Punch a hole in the center and tie a string to a nail; then pull the string through the hole so that the nail is pulled tight against the cardboard.

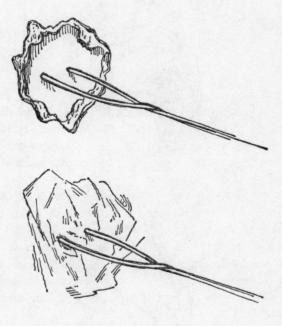

Pass the cardboard through the wall (with the nail on the side away from you) and position it so that the back of the hole is covered. Pull the string taut and tie it to a table leg or chair. Now, build layers of Spackle starting at the cardboard. When the hole has been filled and the Spackle is dry, cut the string at the surface and sand smooth.

Another attack is to crumple newspaper and force it into

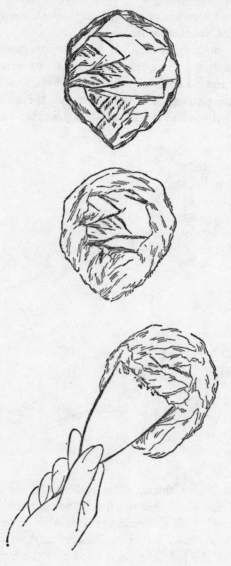

the hole until there is a stable (though not necessarily even) back on which you can spread the first layer of patch and let it dry. In these larger holes, it's best to use patching plaster, which you prepare by mixing with water. Build from there, making the second layer about one-half the thickness of the plaster or gypsum board. When the second coat is perfectly dry, wet it with a sponge (sounds crazy since you just let it dry) and then apply the final coat of patching plaster. If the hole is larger in diameter than your spackling blade (3″), then you'd better beg, borrow, or buy a plasterer's trowel. The blade you use must span the hole so that it can ride on the wall surfaces on either side.[4]

If stuffing newspaper in the hole doesn't appeal to you, cut a piece of heavy cardboard to fit roughly the outline of the hole and wedge it somewhere between the hole's front and back. Glue it in place and then build on that. Be careful! Don't push it all the way through. But if you do, you can always cut and glue another one.

Cracks: Cracks are just long crooked holes. Fill them with the things we've just been talking about.

But, there's a trick to making your crack stay patched. Using a beer can opener (better hang on to it if you have one; it'll be a collector's item before long) or an old beat-up knife blade, dig out the bottom of the crack so that it is larger than the top.

Stop worrying about making the crack larger. Next remove all the loose plaster with an old brush (even better, a vacuum cleaner works wonders) and fill away. With that keystone shape, once the patch hardens you'd have a sweet time getting it out—except by more digging.

Holes in wood: Spackle can even be used on wood. But lots of other hole fillers are available which are used in the same way. Let's look at some of them: *Plastic Wood*—powdered

[4] For holes over 2″ in diameter, the use of patching plaster instead of spackling compound is advised. Patching plaster dries more slowly than spackling compound, but it shrinks less and is stronger.

wood mixed with a quick-drying adhesive. You have to work fast and don't leave the tube or can of the Plastic Wood open. Sand to finish. It has good adhesion and strength. *Linseed oil putty*—really easy to use. Your fingers work best with this one and you don't have to wait for it to dry before painting with an oil base paint. Perhaps not as adhesive as some fillers, it's much used. *Wood putty*—a powder you can mix with water to the consistency of heavy cream. Cheap and handles like Spackle. Good adhesion but must be dry before you paint. *Epoxy putty*—comes in two stiffish sticks. With a knife, cut small, equal slices from each stick and knead the two together thoroughly with a screwdriver or spackling blade. Hardens in a few hours and can be used just about anywhere and on any material (wood, metal, concrete). Expensive, but great. A few people are allergic to epoxy if they handle it.

Holes in masonry: Holes in masonry succumb to treatment using Spackle or epoxy putty, or something called *latex masonry patch* which is very much like cork.

Monster-size holes—up to 3" in diameter: Build a patch in two or more layers. Don't try to fill up the hole all at once! If the large hole is in plaster or gypsum board, use patching plaster or premixed spackling compound, rather than ready-to-mix spackling compound, which shrinks appreciably. If the large hole is in masonry, patching plaster, epoxy putty, or latex masonry patch will all work well.

16

Hanging Things on Walls

Let's begin by dividing things people hang on walls into two groups: Light (weighing up to 5 pounds) and heavy (weighing more than 5 pounds). Use your bathroom scales to weigh what you are going to hang. Sleek, slinky, svelte types who don't even own one of these morale busters take note: Two quarts of milk in a paper carton (or cartons) weigh close to 5 pounds; by comparison estimate the weight of what you want to hang.

FASTENERS FOR LIGHT ITEMS ON HOLLOW WALLS

Most objects hanging on walls weigh less than 5 pounds (pictures, maps, knickknacks, hangings, plates, posters, charts, calendars—ad infinitum). Here are some proper ways to hang them.

Picture Hooks

A metal hook with a nail held at an angle. The old stand-by. These come in an array of sizes, from the smallest, which will safely hold 5 pounds, to the largest, which will support 50 pounds, if it is nailed into a stud. Picture hooks are safe and are usable on any type of wall (except masonry). Place the hook (with nail in place) flat against the wall, and pressing it firmly (no tilt, no slip) hit the nail head firmly with the hammer in line with the direction of the nail. Don't try to murder it. Continue to drive the nail until the hanger fits *just snugly* against the wall; don't beat it into the wall. Remember, the nail goes in at an angle and that's the secret of its holding power. If your wall is plaster, it's less likely to chip at the nail hole if you first glue to the wall a small piece of brown gummed tape or anything held with water-soluble glue. Don't use transparent Scotch tape, adhesive tape, or masking tape; after a while, all will leave water-insoluble guck on your wall, which is a pain to remove.

A picture hook is easy to remove: Place a piece of cardboard or a very thin book *above* the hanger, grip the nail head in the claw of the hammer and *gently* rock the hammer back so that you withdraw the nail at the same angle it went in. If it doesn't want to budge, tap on the end of the hammer handle gently with one hand while holding the handle down with the other. Worry not, you can patch the hole it leaves (see page 156) so that you won't even know it was there.

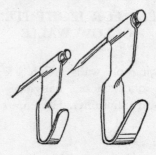

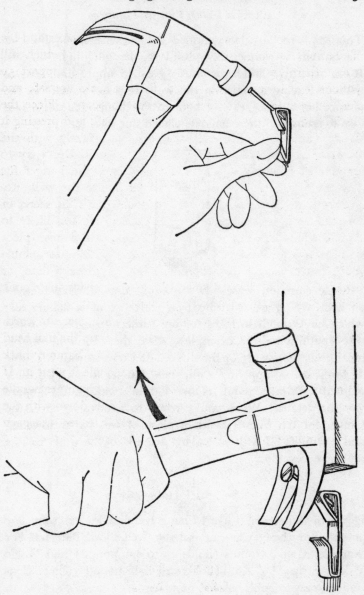

Adhesive Cloth Picture Hangers

This small rectangular gummed hanger with metal hook at the bottom is wonderfully useful for hanging light objects. It's inexpensive and ridiculously easy to apply and remove without leaving a mark on the wall. It is not as safe as the picture hook, but great for lightweight things. It's not a bad idea to use two of these hangers placed side by side.

Some common sense advice: Don't use adhesive hangers on walls which are varnished; on which paint is flaking off; which have rough surfaces; or are subject to excessive moisture (bathrooms, for example). Also, they are *not* suitable for objects that swing or for shelves. It's wise to wait a couple of weeks before applying a glue-held hanger to a wall freshly painted with latex paint. (Once I didn't wait. But I'll spare you the details.) When you're ready to remove it, cover the hanger for ten minutes with a piece of wet paper toweling and it will lift off without leaving a mark on the wall. Sponge off any excess glue.

Self-Stick Hangers

Plenty of things you'd like to hang weigh a lot less than one pound. For these, you can use the "self-stick" hangers. For example, Magic Mounts (holds up to one pound) and Magic Mount Strips, $\frac{1}{2}'' \times 6''$ (holds one-half pound each). Convenient, easy to apply, easy to remove.

If you want to hang small utensils or hot dish pads on a metal cabinet or the stove or the refrigerator, don't overlook the magnetic hooks. They pull right off and stick right back on.

FASTENERS FOR HEAVY ITEMS ON HOLLOW WALLS

Sure, the more secure-type fasteners I am going to tell you about can be used for light objects, but why swat a fly with a sledge hammer? Anyway, it's fun to fit an item to its proper use.

Expansion-Type Fasteners

All expansion fasteners work like this: You drill a hole in the wall, insert the fastener until the front flange is flush with the front wall surface, then the back portion of the fastener is made to expand against the back surface of the wall, resulting in a secure fit. These fasteners come in different sizes but even the smallest will support weights limited primarily by the strength of the wall materials.

This brings us to another subject: The drill. Expansion fasteners are so useful that alone they provide sufficient reason for designating a drill as a "must" tool—to get that necessary hole.

And here we are back to studs again. This time we want to locate the stud not to *use* it but to *avoid* it. Very few things are more maddening than to drill a hole for an expansion fastener—and hit a stud. So, before you drill, check for that stud first! (See page 145.) If you want to hang something at that precise spot over a stud, fine: a picture hook with a nail long enough to penetrate the stud. This will mean a nail between 1½" and 2" long.

Molly Fasteners

These fasteners consist of a "bolt" section and a removable
screw. Using your screwdriver, turn the screw counterclockwise and remove it just to become familiar with the Molly
fastener. Then replace it, screwing it all the way in just until
it stops. From the package determine the proper size hole required and drill it.

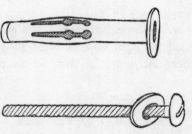

Next, insert the bolt screw combination in the hole you
have drilled and tap it lightly with the hammer.[1] This
completes the insertion of the Molly bolt and embeds the
small points of the cap in the wall. Using your screwdriver
turn the screw clockwise; at first the screw turns easily, then
with more difficulty (keep moderate forward pressure on the
screwdriver as you turn it) as the anchor is pulled back
against the rear surface of the wall. Stop turning when this
operation becomes appreciably more difficult. At this point,
the Molly bolt should be firmly in place. Turn the screw counterclockwise several turns and then try to wiggle the whole
Molly bolt; you shouldn't be able to. Hang anything you
would like on this screw; it may be removed and what's hanging on it interchanged any time the urge strikes you.

When you no longer want to hang anything where there's
a Molly bolt, remove the screw, and, using a hammer and

[1]Molly fasteners with a pointed tip, allowing them to be driven
through plaster or dry wall (gypsum board), are also available. A preliminary hole isn't even necessary. But, don't use one of these unless
you are *positive* there's no stud at that point.

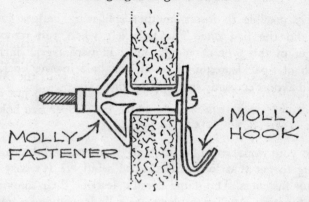

MOLLY
FASTENER

MOLLY
HOOK

either a piece of steel rod screwdriver, or a short piece of wooden dowel the diameter of the Molly bolt head, drive the cap into the wall approximately ⅛". It isn't necessary or desirable to drive the Molly bolt completely through the wall. Next, spackle the hole (see page 156) and, after painting, it disappears from sight and mind.

Toggle Bolt (or Split-Wing or Spring-Wing) Fasteners

These fasteners are very similar to Molly fasteners and are used in precisely the same way. However, there is one difference worth mentioning: Once in place when the screw is removed, the wing part of the hanger falls down behind the hollow wall. This is no serious disadvantage since it is

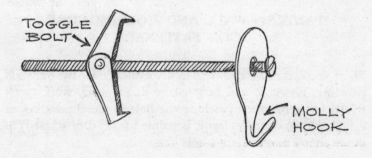

TOGGLE
BOLT

MOLLY
HOOK

always possible to insert another split-wing hanger just as you did the first one. The hole left when you remove a hanger of this type should be filled in two stages, since the depth of Spackle required to fill the hole in one operation would almost certainly crack on drying.

Anchor Fasteners

Have you wondered how to hang a traverse rod from the *ceiling* to get that lusciously draped window? It's easy with anchor fasteners. The name doesn't describe their shape; just their function. Anchor fasteners are cylinders having a tapered hollow center with one end ribbed and split part way along the ribbed section. They are usually made of plastic or lead and come in several sizes. To install this inexpensive, effective hanging device, first drill a hole that just fits the anchor. Insert the anchor, ribbed end first, until the front end is exactly level with the wall surface; then insert a roundhead wood screw and turn it clockwise. The screw spreads the split ribbed sections of the anchor forcing them against the sides of the hole and flaring the ends behind the wall. Directions on the package will specify the proper bit size for drilling the hole and the correct screw size for use with that particular anchor fastener.

PANELED WALL AND HOLLOW-CORE DOOR FASTENERS

Short versions of Molly fasteners are available for use on wood paneling, plywood, and hollow-core doors. They work excellently, but remember, patching the hole in wood paneling or a hollow-core door (unless it is painted instead of stained) is not as simple as spackling a hole in a wall.

FASTENERS FOR MASONRY WALLS

Masonry (poured concrete or concrete block) walls are really thick (8″) and a hole only a fraction of the way through is required for a plastic, lead, or steel anchor, utilizing the same principle as described earlier (page 170).

Check with your hardware salesman the anchor size required for the job you have in mind. Then, from information on the anchor package or the salesman, select the proper size carbide-tipped masonry drill or star drill and have a go at it (see page 152). Before inserting the screw, be sure to seat the anchor firmly in the hole by tapping with a hammer.

Nails? Using a special tool, nails *can* be driven into a masonry wall. However, it's really best to stick to anchors since the holding power of a nail against being pulled out of a masonry wall is poor, and the difficulty of driving it in the first place is great.

HANGING ON THE FASTENERS

I haven't said a word about how to attach the things to be hung to all these wall fasteners. For picture hooks and adhesive cloth picture hangers, the hooks are built right in. For Molly bolts and spring toggle bolts there are only the screw heads and for these it is best to use a little hanger (usually called a Molly hook) which fits right over the screw. Various shapes and sizes are available. For unframed items weighing less than a pound and with a firm backing, attach an adhesive cloth hanger and use its hole to hook into the hanger on the wall.

For framed hangings, the very best system is to use two eye-screws, one on each side of the frame approximately one-quarter of the way from the top. Measure the distances on each side of the frame very carefully so that they will be the same. Then string braided picture wire between the eye-screws. Cut the wire about eight inches longer than the width of the frame and after looping each end twice through its eye, twist the end along the main wire toward the center.

Watch out for those ends! The unraveled tiny wires at the cut end of the braid can prick your finger but good. It's best to use pliers to twist the final inch.

To avoid the sickening sound of a picture frame being split by a screw, use your drill bit to bore a pilot hole (page 151). Make it about three-quarters as deep as you intend to insert the eye-screw—but not all the way through the frame!

HANGING CURTAIN OR TRAVERSE RODS

When you buy fixed or traverse rods, suitable hangers will be supplied which hold the rod at each end. First, position the hangers where you want them and circle inside the screw holes, using a pencil. Measure the distance from your pencil marks to the edge of the window trim and to the ceiling. Adjust the hanger positions until comparable measurements are the *same for both hangers*. (If you reposition a hanger after you've penciled the holes, remember to erase the old marks or they'll foul you up when you bore the pilot holes.)

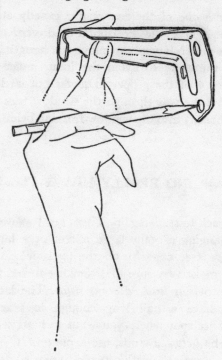

You know better than to use nails to put up curtain or traverse rods, so use screws of the proper diameter (determined by the holes in the hangers) *and length*. If the screws supplied with the hangers are less than ¾″ long, deposit them in your cultch pile[2] and buy new ones.

[2] Webster's Third Unabridged defines "cultch" as: "1a: material (as oyster shells) laid down on oyster grounds to furnish points of attachment for the spat; b: a horny or gelatinous egg mass of a mollusk; 2. *chiefly New England:* TRASH, RUBBISH." All of which shows that Noah and subsequent editors of that august volume were not among the initiated. Do-it-yourselfers quickly collect an invaluable and irreplaceable array of odds and ends without which one is severely handicapped and with which almost *anything* can be fixed. This collection is lovingly referred to as a cultch pile. Trash and rubbish it is not!

This matter is so important that it really deserves more than just a footnote. Saving cultch is the handy person's great secret advantage.

But, suppose one of the screws hits exactly at the corner mitered joint where the horizontal and vertical pieces of window trim meet? If you can move the hanger just enough one way or the other to avoid the joint, great. But if you can't, use screws of the proper diameter but 2″ long so that they will go all the way through the window trim and plaster (or gypsum board) into the window framing behind.

HANGING REALLY HEAVY ITEMS

Now we're back to studs again. There are two ways to tackle the job of hanging a really large mirror or a large picture: Use two large (see capacity on the package) metal picture hangers and make very sure that they are nailed through the wallboard or plaster *into adjacent studs.* The large capacity hanger will have a nail long enough to reach this far. Or, if the exact spot where you want to hang a heavy item turns out to be *between* studs, use a piece of 1″×4″ finished lumber long enough to overlap two adjacent studs and attach the board using two screws reaching into each stud. Be sure the screws are long enough to go through the board, through the wallboard or plaster, and still have 1″ left to penetrate the stud. Hang the heavy object on the board, again using hangers (page 171) secured by screws. You'll like the whole thing better if you lightly sand the edges of the board as well as the surfaces and paint it the color of the wall. Before painting, if you countersink (see page 151) the screws holding it to the studs and fill the holes with Spackle, you will really beam when you show it off.

Be sure a heavy mirror or picture has appropriately sized eye-screws and picture wire.

ADJUSTABLE SHELVES

Impossible to resist since they can be put anywhere. Adjustable shelves can be as tall or as short as you wish and can hold everything from knickknacks to books to an FM receiver and speakers. Not only that, brackets and hangers and shelves can be painted, and prefinished shelves are available in tough, wood-grain finish. And when you move, take 'em with you.

Adjustable shelves are just as easy as anything else to hang using expansion fasteners or screws (if a bracket happens to be over a stud). You'll need two (2) brackets and two (2) hangers for each shelf and for each screw hole a Molly or split-wing fastener (or a 2¼", #9 flathead wood screw for a hole over a stud). If you are making your own shelves, use 1"×8" or 1"×10" clear-grade pine if you plan to stain the shelves; if you're going to paint them, you can use C-select or D-select grades, which are cheaper. Check for warping before you buy the boards, since warped shelves will drive you up the wall every time you look at them.

The *installation:* here goes!

1. Decide where you want the shelves and check to see whether one or more brackets lie over a stud (see page 145).

2. Put the two brackets together to be *sure* they match in every detail from one end to the other—end for end—screw hole for screw hole.

3. To be sure the brackets are straight up and down, tie something (a pencil, a nail—anything) to a piece of string longer than the bracket and tape the free end of the string on the wall alongside the position you will want the bracket. Then line up one of the brackets with the string at the height you want it,

and, with a sharp pencil, carefully circle inside the screw holes on the wall and mark the top and bottom edges of the bracket. An extra pair of helpful hands are mighty useful to keep the bracket from slipping while you mark.

4. Now the *really* important job of lining up the second bracket so that the shelves will be *level*. This means that corresponding holes on one bracket must be the same height from the floor as on the other. Otherwise, slanting shelves. Measure the distance from the floor (or baseboard top) to the bottom mark for the first bracket and make a comparable mark at its position for the second bracket. Do the same for the distance from the ceiling to the top of the brackets.

   Reposition the string and line up the second bracket with it, at the same time checking to see whether the top and bottom ends match the marks on the wall. If so, mark the screw holes and go have something to celebrate your good work. If not, count to ten and remeasure (obviously, your helper let the bracket slip).

5. With your electric drill, bore the appropriate holes (page 148) and hang it up.

17

Happiness Is a
Window That Opens
and a Door That Closes

Windows that stick and doors that scrape are the Athlete's Foot of any household—annoying, irritating, sometimes even painful, but seldom fatal; curable, but rarely cured. Not screaming to be fixed—just whimpering.

A quick trip through this chapter should convince you that many whimpers can be cured in ten minutes or less and need not be left to irritate you. Browse through the ailments of doors and windows and see if you recognize any:

A Casement Window or Jalousie Is Arthritic

Do you remember that marvelous medicine—the silicone spray lubricant—that you discovered in chapter 4? Use it to make any window open more easily.

The point of greatest friction on a crank-operated case-ment window is the track in which the control arm slides.

Spray not only the track, but the top and bottom hinges as well.

Jalousies have a discouragingly high number of points at which two surfaces rub when the window is opened or closed —two spots at each end of each pane. Give each point of friction a short spurt of lubricant to keep it opening smoothly. Failure to lubricate a stiff crank-operated window leads to short-lived crank units. Since exact replacements can be discouragingly difficult to find, regular lubrication is advised.

A Double-Hung (Sash-Type) Window Mistook Your Recent Paint Job for a Glue Job

It's virtually impossible to paint your double-hung windows without sealing them shut, so just plan on Operation Kitchen Knife when the first hot day rolls around after painting. With the thinnest, most flexible kitchen knife you own, slice your way between the sash and the woodwork all the way around the window. If you painted both interior and exterior, you'll have to slice both sides of the sash.

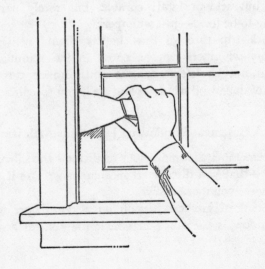

If Operation Kitchen Knife leaves the window still stuck, the next move is Operation Putty Knife; performed from the outside: This lever action from the bottom of the window is easier on both you and the window than pushing and banging it in standard fashion from the inside.

A Window Falls Down on the Job

Double-hung window sashes lift up as easily as they do (although sometimes even they require lubrication) either because they are spring loaded (with a vertical tube on either side of the sash) or because they are counterweighted (with a rope or chain on either side of the sash). If the balance weight is hung by a rope, the rope will eventually break, leaving you either with a repair job or a window requiring a prop to keep it open.

The repair is quite easy to make, once you have purchased sash chain from the hardware store. First, with a broad chisel, remove the wood molding that holds the sash in place.[1] Then pull the sash out of its track, thereby exposing either an opening or a panel covering an opening. Remove the panel to expose the hiding place of the sash counterweight. Replace the old sash rope with new sash chain and reassemble the window. Tack the molding in place with ※4 finishing nails. Set the nails (see page 129) and putty the holes.

A Door Gets the Squeaks

A door squeaks for one of two reasons: either the hinge pins need lubrication, or the doorstop molding at the hinged edge of the door is too snug.

If it's a hinge pin problem, simply fold a newspaper to fit between the floor and the bottom of the door, then remove

[1] Unless the molding is held in place by screws rather than nails, in which case you simply unscrew the molding.

whichever hinge pin is squeaking by tapping upward on a large screwdriver, as shown. Lubricate the pin with a small amount of petroleum jelly or with a squirt of silicone spray, then reinsert the pin in the hinge.

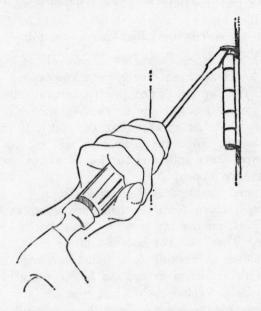

If the squeak squeaks when the door is slightly ajar and is more apparent during humid weather, suspect a doorstop molding which is rubbing the door. (frequently a new coat of paint is enough to render a doorstop too snug.)

First, try spraying the hinged edge of the door with silicone spray. This will work in only perhaps 10% of the cases, but it's so easy that it's worth trying.

If the spray fails, your next step depends on whether your woodwork is varnished or painted.

If it's varnished, pry the doorstop molding off the door frame nearest the hinges with a chisel, remove the nails, move the stop out from the old location about ⅟₁₆″, and renail it, using ⚹6 finishing nails and choosing places where the old nails *weren't*. Set the nails and fill the holes with putty or wood filler that matches your stain.

If it's painted, moving the strip will crack the paint and produce a job that looks rough. You may be able to avoid moving the doorstop molding by removing the door (see page 190 for instructions), and getting it out of the way. Then, using either a multibladed plane (see page 13) or coarse sandpaper on a block of wood, work on the molding until the door no longer rubs.

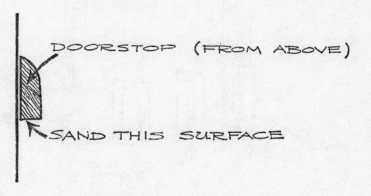

DOORSTOP (FROM ABOVE)

SAND THIS SURFACE

A Door Closes, but Fails to Latch

A door may fail to latch upon closing for one of three reasons. They are:

1. The latch sticks in the "in" position because of friction in the mechanism. The cure for this is discussed on page 29.
2. The distance between the door and the strike plate is greater than the length of the latch. The key word in the cure for this problem is *"Shim* (v.t.)—to change the position of an object by insertion of a thin piece of material between the object and its support; (n.)— the piece of material used to shim an object, usually of

wood, cardboard, or metal." Cardboard makes an ex-
cellent shim in this case.

Remove the strike plate from your door frame by
removing its two screws, and, using it as a template,
cut a piece of cardboard to make an approximate
match. Then reinstall the strike plate with this newly

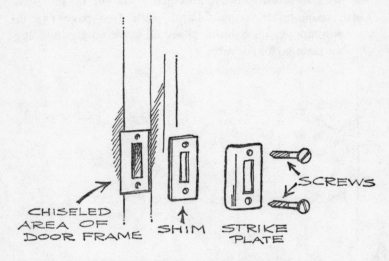

CHISELED
AREA OF
DOOR FRAME   SHIM   STRIKE
PLATE   SCREWS

formed cardboard shim behind it. If one shim doesn't
move the strike plate out far enough to grab the door,
insert one or even two more shims behind the first
one.

When you use two or three layers of cardboard shims,
the chance is high that the screws no longer grab
the wood as firmly as they should. To forestall problems, fill each screw hole with matches or toothpicks
(as described on page 154) before inserting the screws.
If three layers of cardboard still leave you with a
latch that doesn't catch, it's best to move the door

closer to the strike plate by shimming the hinges. Instructions for shimming a hinge are on page 188.

3. It's also possible that your nonlatching door has sagged to the point at which the latch meets the strike plate too low. Or the frame has sagged, and the latch meets the strike plate too high.

If the use of shims fails, and less than ⅛″ stands between you and a working latch, remove the strike plate, hold it firmly in a vise, and enlarge the rectangular hole with a file until the latch can no longer avoid the opening.

In the rare instance that the latch is missing the opening by more than ⅛″, it's advisable to simply move the strike plate up or down. Just follow the pictorial instructions below:

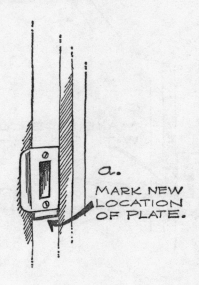

a.

MARK NEW LOCATION OF PLATE.

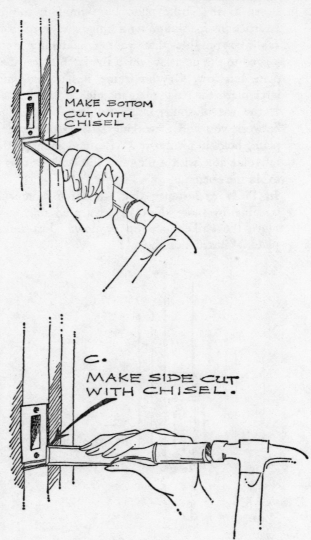

b.
MAKE BOTTOM
CUT WITH
CHISEL

c.
MAKE SIDE CUT
WITH CHISEL.

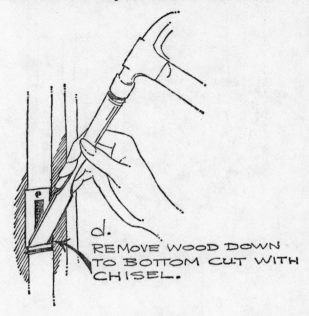

d. REMOVE WOOD DOWN
TO BOTTOM CUT WITH
CHISEL.

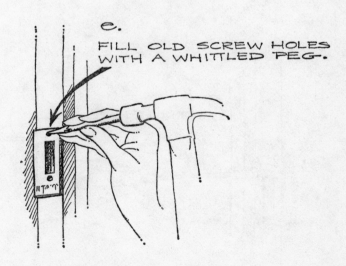

e. FILL OLD SCREW HOLES
WITH A WHITTLED PEG.

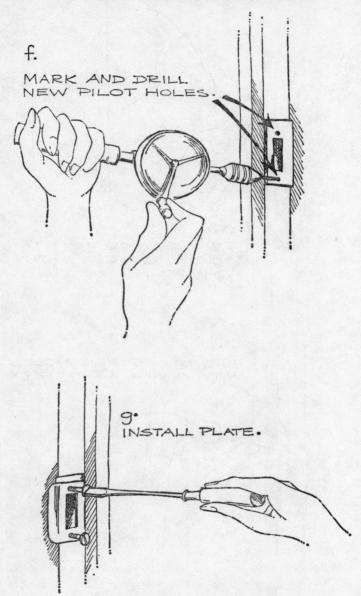

f.

MARK AND DRILL
NEW PILOT HOLES.

g.
INSTALL PLATE.

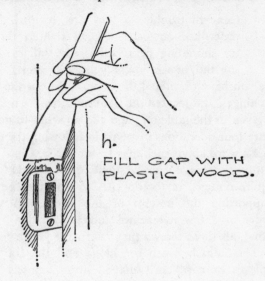

h.

FILL GAP WITH
PLASTIC WOOD.

A Door Sticks, Scrapes, or Refuses to Close Completely

There are three rules to the game of unsticking sticky doors:

Rule #1: Diagnose before you attack. Stand back from the closed door and study the margin between door and frame all the way around the door. Locate the tight spots (look for scratched paint or varnish) and see if there is enough margin on the opposite edge of the door to move the door away from the frame at the tight spots.

Rule #2: Fix the *door*, not the frame. If it becomes necessary to sand or plane, it's the door that takes the gaff, even though it may be straighter than the frame. It's just *easier* to make the door fit the opening than it is to make the opening fit the door.

Rule #3: Always check for tightness of all screws in the hinges first. Loose screws could be the sole cause of trouble; if they are stripped, follow the procedure on page 154 to tighten them. Then try shimming or recessing the hinges; use planing and/or sanding only as a last resort.

Once you have examined the door, ruled out the possibility of loose hinges, and located the tight spots, you're ready for the advice given in the table on page 189 on what to do about it. There are four operations involved in following the table's advice, and a word about each may be useful:

Shimming a hinge can be done quite quickly and does not require removal of the door. After opening the door 90° and supporting the bottom of the door with yesterday's newspaper or a few magazines, loosen partially (about two full turns) all three screws that fasten the hinge to the door frame. Then slip between the hinge and the frame one or more pieces of cardboard shaped approximately like this:

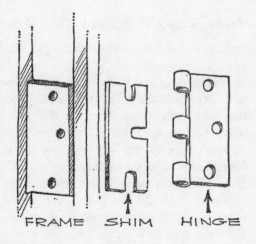

FRAME   SHIM   HINGE

Then tighten the screws and try the door.

If more than one cardboard shim has been used, it may be necessary to apply the stripped screw treatment to the screws as described on page 154. Treat one screw at a time to keep the hinge in place.

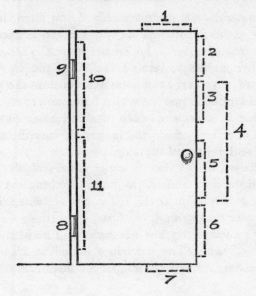

Table

Procedures for Relieving Tight Spots on a Door
(Numbers refer to the figure above.)

Tight Spot	First try to shim at:	Then try to recess at:	As last resort, plane or sand at:
1 and/or 6	9	8	1 and/or 6
2 and/or 7	8	9	2 and/or 7
3	—	9	10—then recess at 9
5	—	8	11—then recess at 8
4 or any combination of 2 or 3 with 5 or 6	—	8 and 9	10 and 11—then recess at 8 and 9

Removing a door is necessary only if you intend to recess a hinge or plane the door. First, support the bottom of the door with magazines or a folded newspaper. Then, starting with the *bottom hinge,* remove the hinge pin by wedging the blade of your largest screwdriver beneath the head of the pin and tapping it upward with a hammer.

When you have removed both pins and have wiggled and pulled the door away from the hinges, be careful not to hit the ceiling with the top of the door.

Reinstallation of the door is easily done with two people, one to hold the door and one to guide together the two parts of each hinge and slip in the hinge pin (lubricate it first). Always replace the top hinge pin first.

Recessing a hinge requires a hammer and a chisel between ¾″ and 1¼″ wide. The procedure is one which you may want to practice on a piece of scrap wood first:

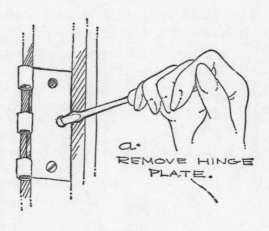

a.
REMOVE HINGE
PLATE.

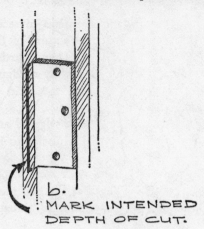

b.
MARK INTENDED
DEPTH OF CUT.

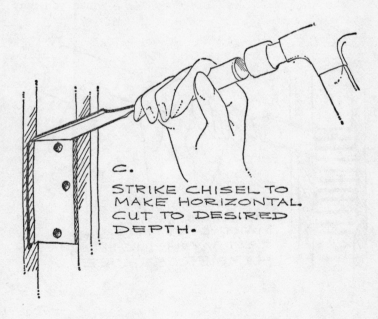

c.
STRIKE CHISEL TO
MAKE HORIZONTAL
CUT TO DESIRED
DEPTH.

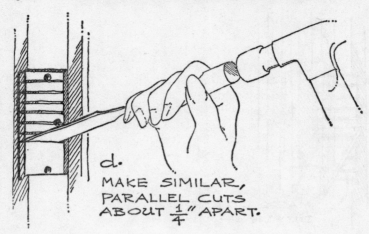

d.
MAKE SIMILAR,
PARALLEL CUTS
ABOUT $\frac{1}{4}$" APART.

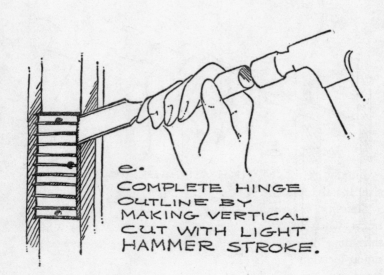

e.
COMPLETE HINGE
OUTLINE BY
MAKING VERTICAL
CUT WITH LIGHT
HAMMER STROKE.

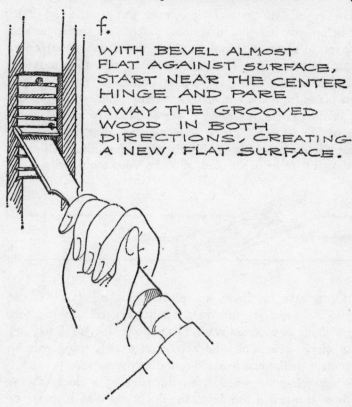

f.

WITH BEVEL ALMOST
FLAT AGAINST SURFACE,
START NEAR THE CENTER
HINGE AND PARE
AWAY THE GROOVED
WOOD IN BOTH
DIRECTIONS, CREATING
A NEW, FLAT SURFACE.

Finally, reinstall the hinge plate and try the door on for size. Install top hinge pin first.

Sanding or planing should generally be used as a last resort, when it's obvious that the door can't be made to fit by shimming or recessing the hinges alone. Unless you're sanding at location (1), (2), or (6) in the figure on page 189, removal of the door is necessary, and an assistant is recommended to hold the door while you work on it.

Planing will do the nicest job, once you get the feel of it; but before planing your first door, practice on the edges and ends of a piece of scrap lumber. You'll quickly discover that it's better to have the blade set too shallow than too deep and that when planing the top or bottom of the door, you *must* plane from the corner to the center, but, when planing the vertical edges, it's often better to plane from the center toward the corner. You'll also discover that cocking the plane slightly askew from the direction of motion (although holding it flat) helps the blade slice the wood more easily.

If you have no plane or multibladed plane (such as the easy-to-use Stanley Surform), sandpaper will do the job. Use a coarse or medium grade (40 to 80 grit or ⚒ 1½ to ⚒ 0) on a block or orbital sander (see page 16), using care to keep the edge flat and to avoid rounding the corners.

When removing wood from the edge of a door, *always* mark with a pencil the depth to which you wish to plane or sand, unless the door is still on its hinges and, therefore, subject to constant checking.

An Exterior Door Provides Unwanted Air Conditioning in the Winter

All exterior doors in houses requiring heat in the winter should be weather stripped. You'll find, at your hardware store, as many as a half-dozen different kinds of weather stripping to do this job; each type, without exception, has its own specific disadvantage. On the basis of effectiveness, appearance, convenience, length of life, and ease of installation, I recommend the following:

For doors that fit well in their frames ($\frac{1}{16}''$ to $\frac{1}{8}''$ margin between door and frame), spring bronze stripping is preferred. It is used on all but the bottom of the door and is easily installed on the door frame in an inconspicuous location.

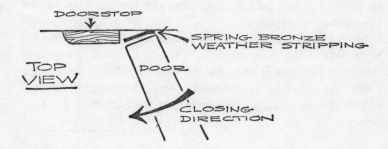

For doors with more than $\frac{1}{8}''$ or less than $\frac{1}{32}''$ margin between door and frame at some point, a Neoprene strip nailed to the doorstop does the best job. Nail it in place with the door in the closed position:

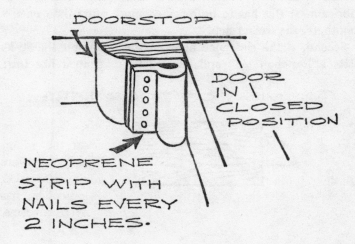

A Door Lock Fails to Function Smoothly

If your door lock is acting as if it is ready for retirement, you'll be cheered to know that silicone spray lubricant is a veritable Fountain of Youth for arthritic locks and latches. As a first effort, simply spray lubricant into the keyhole and onto every sliding surface, including the key itself, and work the mechanism repeatedly.

If this produces no change, locate the screws on the interior side of the door which hold the lock assembly together, remove them, and disassemble the assembly. With the interior knob and cover plate removed, spray the internal surfaces of the lock mechanism while you turn the lock from the outside.

A Door Fails to Close Smoothly Unless It's Slammed or Its Knob Is Turned

There are four separate actions to take in licking this problem; start with the easiest and quit when you've conquered.

First, just spray the latch and strike plate with silicone lubricant. If this has to be repeated more often than once a month, try the second step.

Second, if the clearance between the door and the strike plate is less than ⅛″, and if the latch is shaped like this:

TOP VIEW OF DOOR LATCH:

rather than like this:

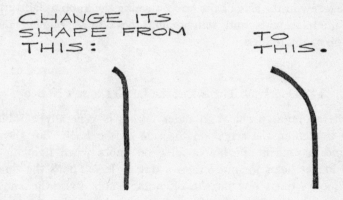

try bending the strike plate a little. Put the strike plate into a vise and, by tapping lightly with a hammer

Third, if changing the shape of the strike plate didn't help or wasn't appropriate, dismantle the doorknob completely and spray everything that moves with silicone lubricant. Doorknob dismantling procedure is described on page 198.

Fourth, if, after reassembly of the doorknob and latch unit, smooth operation is still not permanently attainable, the time has arrived for a new doorknob and latch set.

Friction in Your Doorknob Makes the Latch Stick in the Open Position

Owners of homes equipped with "economy" doorknob sets will find this problem appearing after about seven years of use and should recognize it as a signal to begin replacing the cheap sets with better ones. Don't spend money immediately, however. First try dismantling the unit and giving everything a silicone spray. If that fails, buy the new set after reading about latch set replacement below.

If you live in a house old enough to have "skeleton key"-type locks on each door, friction in the doorknob could be related to the problem discussed in the next paragraph. Try loosening the screw in the side of the knob, turning the knob a half turn counterclockwise, and retightening the screw, wiggling the knob as you tighten.

The Doorknob Turns, but the Latch Doesn't Notice

This common problem in older homes is generally curable by tightening the screw on the side of the knob. But there comes a time in the life of all good knobs when tightening no longer helps for more than a day or less. That's the time to loosen the screw on the offending knob, twist the knob counterclockwise until it comes off its threaded stem, and observe that the stem is pretty thoroughly chewed up. Procure a new stem from the hardware store and, after giving the works a blast of silicone spray, thread everything back together.

Removing and Replacing a Door Latch Assembly

There are two types of doorknob units. The "mortise-type" set is found in all older homes (prior to 1946), and, with occasional lubrication, can be expected to last forty years or more. The "cylindrical-type" set, which is much more quickly and easily installed, is now used almost exclusively and appears in most homes built after 1946.

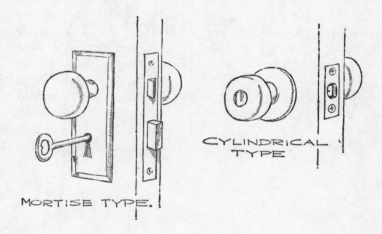

MORTISE TYPE.

CYLINDRICAL TYPE

To remove a mortise-type set, loosen (but don't remove) the screw on the side of the knob, then unscrew the knob and remove the other knob by pulling it out. Unscrew all other screws in sight, removing the cover panels in the process (don't forget the two screws in the panel containing the latch); then slide the unit out through the edge of the door. Its replacement can be installed by running this paragraph backward.

Removal of most cylindrical sets involves unscrewing the two screws in the decorative escutcheon plate around the knob on one side of the door and pulling both knobs out of the door; removal of the two screws in the latch plate will then make it possible to slide the latch unit out through the edge of the door. A new set goes in by running the procedure backward.

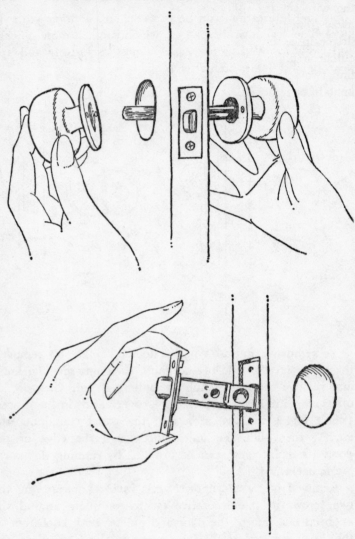

Some latch sets have no screws on either escutcheon
plate; rather the knob on one side is held in place by a
spring-loaded wire reaching out through a slot in the neck
of the knob. With the blade of a small screwdriver press

the wire toward the center of the knob and pull the knob
away from the door. With the knob removed, slip the screwdriver in a slot which you will find in the rim of the escutcheon plate and pry the plate loose. Beneath it you will
find two screws which, when removed, will allow the other
knob to be removed.

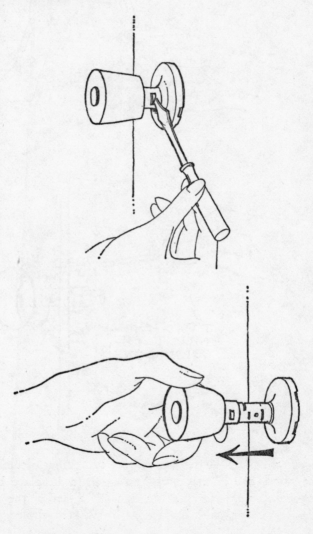

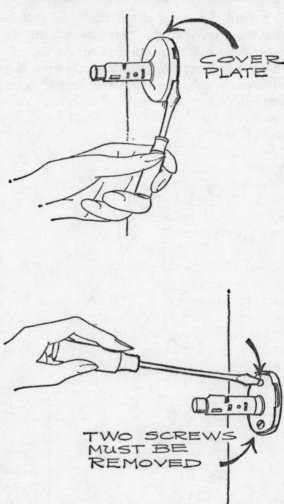

COVER
PLATE

TWO SCREWS
MUST BE
REMOVED

Cupboard Doors Won't Stay Closed

If you have a malfunctioning latch on a cupboard door that a little bit of screw tightening and adjusting doesn't cure, smile broadly. Because you now have a perfect excuse to run to the hardware store for one of those neat, eternally trouble-free magnetic catches that every cabinet should have. These wonderful devices consist of just a magnet (usually on the cabinet) and a metal plate (usually on the door); you can install one yourself quite easily.

If the cabinet has a second door, open that, and, by reaching through the second door, put the magnet, with metal piece attached, into the desired position against the closed door receiving the new latch. Then, without moving the magnet, open the door and with a pencil mark the location of the screw holes. Following the advice proffered on page 151 about screws and pilot holes, install the magnet. Once more, with door closed, mark the location of the metal plate and then, with door open, drill a pilot hole and install the plate. But watch it! *Don't drill all the way through the door!* Put a piece of adhesive tape around the drill bit to indicate the proper depth to drill.

Unless, like Alice, you find a little three-legged table, all made of solid glass, and on it a bottle with a paper label with the words DRINK ME beautifully printed in large letters, most cabinets with only one door present a real problem; it's pretty tricky to get the door closed with your hand inside holding the magnet.

Here's the next best way: Put the metal piece on the magnet and install the magnet so the metal plate is flush with the cabinet edge. Then remove the plate, put its screw (or screws) through the hole (or holes) and, with the point of the screw facing you, snap the plate back in position on the magnet. The close the door just forcefully enough to make the screw

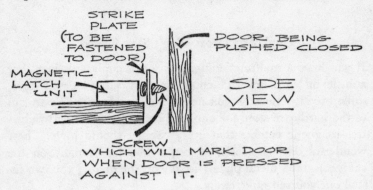

STRIKE
PLATE
(TO BE
FASTENED
TO DOOR)

DOOR BEING
PUSHED CLOSED

MAGNETIC
LATCH
UNIT

SIDE
VIEW

SCREW
WHICH WILL MARK DOOR
WHEN DOOR IS PRESSED
AGAINST IT.

tip scratch the inside surface of the door. The scratch becomes
the mark for your pilot hole. Don't forget to tape the drill bit
to regulate the depth of the holes you drill!

18

If You Aspire to Greater Heights—Use a Ladder

Selecting a Ladder

Aluminum ladders are light, strong, won't rust, and can be stored outside if necessary. That's for you. But how long should a ladder be? If your house is one story, a single-piece ladder should be perfect and should be about two to three feet longer than the distance from the gutter to the ground. Before you go to the hardware store, find out how far that is by extending your six-foot folding rule all the way and hold it up until it touches the gutter, noting the position of the bottom end against the house. Then measure from there to the ground and add the two.

Before you buy the ladder, pick it up and try erecting it against the outside wall of the store (see below). Don't buy a ladder you can't handle. A two-story house requires an extension ladder, which, even in aluminum, will be heavy. Thoroughly check out with the hardware salesman your ability to handle an extension ladder of the necessary length.

Erecting a Ladder

1. Against a roof with very little or no overhang: Place the ladder on the ground with the bottom end against the house foundation. Standing at the other end and facing the house, raise the ladder with both hands, and holding it above your head, "walk-it-up" a rung at a time until the top rests against the house. With one hand on a rung above your head keeping the ladder pressed against the house and the other hand on a lower rung lift the bottom end and slide it about two feet away from the house. Now slide the bottom again until its distance from the house is one-fourth the length of the ladder. If the ladder is twisted, adjust it until it lies flat against the gutter or roof edge. You now have the arrangement of maximum stability and safety.

2. Against a roof with overhang, this is a job for *you and a friend*. Lay the ladder on the ground perpendicular to the house with the bottom end just outside the overhang line. Ask your friend to kneel and grasp both sides near the bottom and press down while you raise the ladder by "walking-it-up" rung by rung with your hands above your head (see above). With the ladder pressed against the gutter (or roof edge), lift slightly and slide the bottom until its distance from the overhang line is one-fourth the length of the ladder.

Moving a Ladder

Just a few feet: Standing at the foot of a ladder, facing the house, slide the top about a foot, then lift the ladder enough to slide the bottom the same distance and in the same direction so that the ladder is now resting firmly on both feet. Repeat until you are where you want to be, but don't try to slide it too far in any one move.

A long distance: Take the ladder down, reversing the steps used to raise it.

Some More Do's That Add Up to Safety

1. Before you get on a ladder, be sure that the two end pieces are firmly placed on the ground. Holding onto higher rungs, jump up and down once or twice on the bottom rung to seat the ladder.

2. If the ladder is resting on asphalt or concrete, or any surface where it might slip, *always* have someone else hold the ladder with both hands and with both feet planted against the bottom ends.

3. When you're on the ladder, work only within an arm's length on either side. Keep your whole body between the two ladder sides, and if you can't reach something, get down and move the ladder to a new location.

Stepladders

About standing on tables and chairs: NO, NO, NO! Nothing takes the place of a good stepladder. But how do you tell a good stepladder from a dangerous one?

A 5′ stepladder is just about right for anything you encounter in the house. It should be aluminum and the two legs holding the steps should be not less than 18″ apart at the floor. The front legs and the steps should be at least 3″ wide and, when erected, the distance between the front and back legs of the ladder should be not less than 30″. There *must* be two locking braces (one on each side) between the front and back legs, a paint shelf that folds down, and rubber pads on the leg bottoms. The thicker the aluminum the better.

My stepladder has a label with the following suggestions:

1. Open the ladder fully and snap the spreader bars firmly into place.
2. Place the ladder near the work to be done.
3. Face the ladder at all times.
4. Work within arm's reach with the body over the ladder.
5. Do not stand on the *paint shelf* or the *top of the ladder*.

And I would add—

6. Use the ladder outside only on a smooth, flat surface.

Cleaning gutters: Are you queasy about heights and do you get a hollow feeling inside when you think of climbing to the roof? Then don't; get someone else to do it. However, if you are a climber and you have a one-story house, you will need a metal or wood ladder (not a stepladder) that'll reach the gutters easily. Be smart, and use the ladder correctly and safely (see page 207).

The best time to clean gutters is after all the leaves are off the trees and, in spite of what you may think when you climb up the ladder, they are not all in your gutters. Don't forget to squirt the hose in the gutter (or up on the roof) and watch the downspout to be sure it isn't plugged up. If it is, with the hose going full-blast through a nozzle set for its most penetrating stream, push the hose down the clogged drainspout. When all else fails, buy some galvanized wire (comparable in size to that used in coat hangers), bend a hook at the end, and fish out the obstruction (leaves).

19

Humidity

GOOD, BAD, AND RELATIVE

The trouble with humidity is that it's just about never what it ought to be: too high in the summer (and all year around in some basements), too low in winter.

Too much humidity: With central air conditioning you don't sweat too much about humidity, unless you have a leaky basement. Even air conditioning won't make that go away. Have you ever been in a basement that's so damp and moldy that it makes your skin crawl? How to handle wet basements depends upon just how bad the situation really is.

If there's no evidence of wet walls or floors but there's still dampness, is your clothes dryer vented to the outside? A common source of too much moisture in a basement is a clothes dryer that is vented directly into it. There are two things wrong with this arrangement: Too much water vapor is dumped into the air all at once, and along with it goes fine lint particles which make a mess by settling all over the place. Moral: Place your dryer so that it can be vented through a window (easy for you to do) or have a vent put in the basement wall (expensive since somebody else will have to do it). While we're talking about dryers, remember to disassemble the vent tube (it's easy since it's put together with slip joints which may or may not be taped) and clean out the collected lint once a year to prevent overheating and damage to the dryer. But clean the lint trap after every load.

A great answer to non-wet but humid basements is an electric dehumidifier, essentially a tiny, relatively inexpensive, refrigeration unit (about 12″×12″×20″). Moisture is removed from the air by condensation on cold coils. An automatic sensor (humidistat) tells the dehumidifier when to run and when to cut off. The unit comes with a pan to catch the water, but unless you're strange and unusual you'll never remember to empty the pan before you have to mop up the floor. Solution: put the dehumidifier on a shelf or a table or brackets above the level of the laundry tub (or sump pump) with a hose or pipe leading directly to the drain. Then turn it on and forget it. As a permanent arrangement you can also forget the chemical, crystal dehumidifiers for use in a wet basement. They don't have the necessary capacity and have to be either rejuvenated or changed constantly.

Big trouble you really have if there's water on the floor or wet areas on the basement walls or floors. First check the drainage around the house during and after the next heavy rain. The ground should slope *away* from the foundation to carry off the water. Prescription for a nightmare: Ground sloping toward the foundation along with stopped-up gutters or those that empty too near the house. But all can be corrected.

If you decide that the slope of the ground should be changed or that installation of gutters is necessary, call for professional help (see "Contractors—Grading" or "Roofing Contractors" in the Yellow Pages). If you suspect that your gutters need cleaning, you can check and clean them yourself after reading page 208 and chapter 18 on the use of ladders.

If none of the above helps and it's obvious that water is

entering the basement at a crack in the corner or at the base of a wall where it joins the floor, clean the area with a wire brush (hardware store) and fill the crack with quick-set cement or some other suitable cement crack filler of which there are a number available. When the wall and filler are dry, apply a coat of epoxy resin sealer (paint or hardware store) and then a second coat according to the directions. Be sure there's plenty of ventilation when you use epoxy or any other non-water base paint. You can paint the whole basement with epoxy if you wish, but it's not cheap. But it *is* waterproof and tough.

Now, for the last resort—and the only really *sure* cure for wet basements. Have a trench dug around the house foundation down to the footings. Clean the foundation wall and apply a coat of asphalt cement and a layer of heavy plastic or other waterproof sheeting. Then lay drain tile and replace the dirt. Look in the Yellow Pages under "Waterproofing Contractors" for someone who does this kind of work. Of course, all this *should* have been done when the house was built.

House-Buying Advice: When you're house hunting and find the perfect one, except that it has a basement which is wet or damp or has a musty odor, run as hard as you can—in the opposite direction. (Unless, of course, you're prepared to add to the price of the house the cost of the project described above.)

Too little humidity: Is your skin dry and scaly, do the mucous membranes inside your nose feel like parchment, and are you chilly even though the thermostat is turned up to the right temperature? Yep, that's low humidity. The proper amount of moisture in the air allows your skin to be moist and to function normally and you to feel warmer at a *lower* temperature (the lower fuel bill will warm your bank account, too).

And what should the relative humidity inside be in the

winter? Between 15 and 35%, depending upon the outside temperature. And what is it without humidification? Commonly as low as 5%. Cracks open up in the floor, joints in molding appear—all from shrinkage of wood losing moisture in the low humidity.

The one and only cure is more good old H_2O in the air, and the surprising part is the tremendous quantity required to bring the relative humidity up to par. It really isn't practical to leave the hot shower on, or to have someone run continuously through the house waving a steaming towel, or to keep the kettle whistling on the stove, even if they would do the job. But there are other ways:

In houses with old-fashioned hot water or steam radiators, a water pan (designed especially for this use) on each will do a better-than-nothing job *if kept filled*. Floor unit humidifiers are readily available and are the only type satisfactory for non-forced heating systems. Be sure the capacity matches the size of your house.

Forced-air heating systems are the most adaptable of all to humidity control since there is a built-in distribution system. But there are humidifiers and there are humidifiers. This really is an area in which you get what you pay for. Just putting any old humidifier in the air ducts of the heating system will *not* be satisfactory. Stick to a nationally advertised brand and have a reputable contractor install the unit with *sufficient capacity* to be satisfactory. He will need to know the size of your house, the type of insulation, whether you have storm windows, and perhaps more.

But, *note:* Sad to say, all houses can't be humidified successfully; those well-built within the past twenty years generally can be, but your contractor should check to be sure not only that the house is insulated but that the insulation used incorporates a vapor barrier (sheet aluminum foil, plastic, or waterproof paper). If your house qualifies and you have it humidified, that will be some of the best money you ever spent.

20

Maybe That Dead Appliance Is Only Sick

I can sympathize with appliance manufacturers.

The perfect appliance (be it a toaster, a mixer, or a shaver) should have the following properties:

1. Effectiveness
2. Convenience
3. Reliability and ruggedness
4. Attractiveness
5. Safety
6. Ease of storage and maintenance
7. Minimum cost
8. Compactness
9. Long life
10. Ease of repair

To get all ten of these properties into a single package obviously takes something close to genius, and I'll admit to being impressed with the high scores most small appliances make on this check list; nevertheless, every appliance marketed represents a compromise among these ten properties.

Now, tell me the truth: If you were marketing food blenders, which of these ten properties would you sacrifice first?

Let me give you a clue. Could you conceive of a conversation like this at the Blender Counter?

"This green one looks pretty substantial, Marcia."

"Yes, John, and I like the convenience of pushbuttons. But I hear that if one of those clever pushbuttons goes bad, you have to replace all eleven switches. No, better not get that one."

"How about this beautiful harvest-gold unit with thirteen speeds? Good price too."

"Oh John, don't be ridiculous! The on-off switch is riveted to the case and would be the devil to replace. How about this one?"

"That orange thing in the wooden case? Have you been sniffing carburetor cleaner again, Marcia?"

"No, John—this ticket says that I can replace the brushes on the motor of this blender with only a screwdriver in less than eight minutes. What more could we want?"

"I guess you're right, Marcia—we'll get that one."

Ease of repair is not only the least marketable feature, it also often competes against safety and compactness. Little wonder, then, that most appliances sold are often about as easy to fix as a broken egg yolk. Not all repairs on all appliances are impossible, however, and this chapter contains suggestions for handling the easily cured problems.

Nearly half of all appliance problems involve a break in the electric cord, which is usually a routine job. Another 20% involve something else that's fixable, so you can expect to aim for a 50 to 70% success rate on your appliance repair efforts.

How to detect a break in the electric cord: Give it the Eagle Eye. X-ray vision would be mighty handy at this point but you can sometimes come pretty close to it by carefully examining the wire where it enters the plug and where it enters the appliance. Does it seem to be unusually flexible and floppy at one of these points? Does a gentle tug make it feel more stretchy than the rest of the wire? Is the wire so old that the insulation has lost flexibility and cracks in the insulation are beginning to appear at the ends of the wire? If the answer is "yes" to any of these, your diagnosis is probably complete, but if it's "no," it still may be a broken wire.

Try the Squeeze Play. A break in a wire would, of course, look to a believer in X-ray vision something like this:

INSULATOR
CONDUCTOR

LAMP CORD
SECTION:

And, by judicious lengthwise compression of the wire, you may, temporarily, be able to reunite the two broken strands, like this:

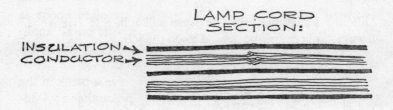

LAMP CORD
SECTION:

INSULATION
CONDUCTOR

If your appliance sputters to a start, you've got the problem located. (You may even be able to use this as a temporary repair measure in an emergency.) But if it doesn't sputter to a start, it's still possible that you have a broken cord on your hands.

Try the Last Resort. After reading the words of wisdom on page 219 about taking things apart, open the appliance and remove the cord. Often the most difficult part of this job is freeing the cord from the outer shell of the unit because of the pesky grommet that holds it in place:

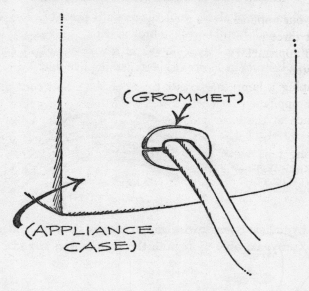

(GROMMET)

(APPLIANCE
CASE)

Although sometimes finger pressure will suffice to remove the
grommet, pliers may be needed to do the job:

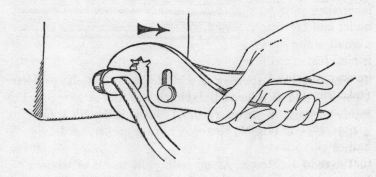

If the grommet should crack when you're removing it, don't
lose heart—you'll probably be able to wedge the pieces back
in place later and never notice the difference; if not, replace
it at the hardware store.

If your appliance uses a grounded plug (see page 71), one of the three wires in your cord will be attached to some part of the appliance casing. Mark this wire, then ignore it in the next step.

Unplug a lamp and create for it an extension cord made of the appliance cord which you have just removed by taping each of the bare wire ends of the cord onto one of the prongs of the lamp plug. Adhesive tape is best, but plastic mending tape will work too. Make certain that there is no metal-to-metal contact except for the contact with each wire beneath the tape.

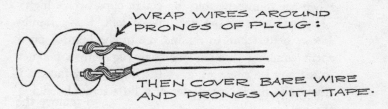

WRAP WIRES AROUND PRONGS OF PLUG:

THEN COVER BARE WIRE AND PRONGS WITH TAPE.

Lay this ridiculous-looking assembly on a wood or cloth surface; then plug your erstwhile appliance cord into the wall outlet and turn on the lamp. If it fails to light, allow yourself a small, smug sneer at the offending wire, for you have found it out. Just remember to pull the plug out of the wall before unwrapping the tape! Buy yourself some new wire and plug (take the old wire with you to the hardware store just to play safe), consult page 85, and you're on your way.

But what if it isn't the wire? My statement that almost half of all appliance problems involve the electric cord means that over half of the problems *aren't* caused by the cord, and I regret to admit that in these cases the going is tougher, the guidelines are fewer, and, in some cases, the path is intentionally blocked by the manufacturer.

But—this is not the time to throw that unco-operative appliance away! You owe it to yourself and to that inanimate technological failure whose wire you hold to remember those three gems of wisdom propounded by seasoned handymen:

1. Sometimes the appliance shapes up and works simply by being dismantled and reassembled.
2. You can't make the appliance any worse—it's ready for the trash can right now.
3. Browsing around through the inner being of that appliance is the only way to learn.

BUT, before you browse, here are three important reminders:

1. Never, *never* browse with the plug in the socket!
2. Remember the sage advice offered by my mother when she found me stacking coffee cups twelve high: "If anything *can* fall or spill—it *will*."[1] My family knows better than to remind me of the hours I once spent combing through our shag rug with a magnet in search of a tiny spring, or the look on my face as I listened to the merry clatter of a little screw bouncing through the hot air register in our kitchen floor, or the interesting remarks I made after a link from a watchband slithered neatly into the inaccessible bowels of our sofa.[2] Pay heed to the sotto voce of sad experience and open your appliances on a flat surface, comfortably far from inviting holes, cracks, and crevices. Better yet, work on a cookie sheet with shallow sides, and use an egg carton to store the nuts, bolts, and miscellaneous parts.
3. Make notes to yourself as you disassemble. Drop each set of screws into a different hole in the egg carton— then add a scrap of paper with a note about their

---

[1] Actually, this sage advice was delivered very rapidly and at the top of her lungs; the coffee cups proved her point within a second of her exposition of her thesis.

[2] This paragraph is simply an application of a well-known scientific law, which in its most elegant form is stated, "Falling toast always lands jelly side down."

origin. Before you pull something loose, draw a picture that will be enough to prevent your replacing it backward. Disassemble the item carefully and observantly, and the reassembly will be easy.

When I tear into an ailing appliance, there is a general approach I consistently use, and I recommend it to you:

1. In order to get the case or cover off, make the assumption that every screw left exposed by the manufacturer holds the case on; even if it doesn't, it generally won't hurt to unscrew it anyway.

2. Once you have everything pretty well exposed, look around for:

(a) A loose or broken wire.

(b) A loose nut or bolt, or a part that looks as if it has shifted its position recently (often detectable by a spot not covered with dust or grease).

(c) A blackened spot caused by a short circuit (this may indicate a loose wire, which is easily cured, but may also mean that the motor or heater is defunct, which is seldom worth curing).

(d) Evidence that the switch is faulty, indicated by the presence of corrosion (which can be removed by a nail file or an emery board along with some care and patience), or by undue stiffness in the action (which calls for a couple shots of the silicone lubricant mentioned in chapter 4).

(e) A lubrication problem either in the motor bearings or in some other mechanical part. (As I've said before: When in doubt—spray a shot of lubricant.)

(f) Evidence that dirt or food has made something stick or work hard. (If the problem is food, then spray lubricant does little or nothing—a spray detergent or concentrated detergent solution and a tooth pick or toothbrush is needed.)

If, after looking, poking, scratching, probing, wiggling,

loosening, tightening, twisting, and turning every likely part inside that case, whether you find something suspicious or not, the thought will finally occur to you:

"Is it safe to try to run the appliance with the case off or open?" No question about it—you'll learn a lot by trying it. But is it safe? The answer is "Yes—*if*":

1. You take it off that metal cookie sheet you're using. It should be safely away from all conducting surfaces.

2. You adopt the time-honored rule of TV repairmen: When a unit is plugged in, always work with one hand in your pocket, keeping your distance from any conductor such as a metal table, a concrete floor, or any moisture. The idea, of course, is to avoid making yourself any part of an electrical loop, especially to make it impossible for current to flow up one arm, through any part of your torso, and down a leg or another arm. If you follow the one-hand rule, and you do get a shock, the loop through you will probably involve only a part of one hand and (apart from the surprise and discomfort) no damage will be done.

3. You make sure that moving parts are still free to do their thing without striking anything.

4. You are ready to yank the plug with great alacrity if something unsuspected and untoward should occur.

Figure on a success rate of about one out of three or four for appliances with troubles other than defective cords. Even at this modest rate your savings will be significant—and with a little experience and perseverence you'll soon have your batting average up to .400 or .500!

21

Diagnosing Ailments of Specific Appliances

It would be lovely if I could, in a couple of fact-filled chapters, give you explicit instructions for curing all common ailments in all the common appliances, but it can't be done even in ten chapters, simply because the game of locating and repairing a malfunction much more resembles a fox hunt than a square dance. Nevertheless, there are numerous bits of advice worth dispensing, arranged here according to the type of appliance.

Battery-powered carving knives, toothbrushes, and shavers: If the unit worked perfectly last time and is dead this time, suspect the wall-mounted charging unit. If the unit recently seemed to have been filled with tired blood, suspect that the batteries will no longer hold a charge. But don't jump to any conclusions until you have looked at the contacts (pull the plug first) between holder and appliance: often the problem is nothing more than grimy contacts, and a cotton swab with rubbing alcohol is all that's needed. Battery-powered units are usually designed to make battery replacement difficult, if not impossible, and burned out charger units are not worth repairing. If the problem isn't dirt, resign yourself to discarding the entire unit.

Blenders, electric: Three things are likely to cause trouble in an electric blender: failure of the speed selection switch unit, wearing of the motor bearings or brushes (sliding contacts made of graphite), and severe wearing of the vertical, spinning power shaft and/or mixing blade unit. Switch failure will cause the motor to spark and run at incorrect speeds on some settings. Bearing failure and worn brushes will cause the motor to spark and make vicious noises at any speed. Power shaft or mixing blade failure will produce unpleasant noises, too, but only with the blender jar in place. Unfortunately, these units are not made to be repaired, and parts are difficult to procure. Try to diagnose the malfunction, call a repair center that handles your brand, get an estimate—but be prepared to buy a new unit. Before you discard the old one, take it apart and examine both motor and switch unit.

Can openers, electric: These devices are clearly a technological retreat, rather than an advance. No longer hung conveniently on the wall, they occupy valuable counter space, get pushed around, tipped over, and spilled upon. Inconvenient to use with tall cans and helpless in a power failure, they have made it necessary for every home to have a small, hand-operated can opener for emergencies. The only reason they sell so well is that the American game of musical houses is so pervasive that no one lives in a given house long enough to install a wall-mounted can opener; besides, if one were to miss the stud in the installation process (see page 145), many of the walls in new apartment complexes would be too weak to support a wall-mounted opener.

The death potion for these devices is the juice of the cans on which they grind. A splash and a dribble at a time, the syrups and sauces work their sticky way into the kinks and crannies of the mechanism, gluing, rusting, and corroding parts that used to slide freely and easily. Hence, the appropriate preventive medicine is frequent, routine cleaning, and the best cure of a balky unit is disassembly and thorough cleaning, followed by lubrication of all moving parts. The manufacturer, you'll notice, uses grease for this purpose. Vaseline (petroleum jelly) is a good substitute and, of course, is completely nontoxic.

Carving knives, battery powered: See battery-powered carving knives, toothbrushes, and shavers.

Food mixers, counter-top: The large, stand-supported food mixers that sell for $45 and up represent a sizable investment, but they are rugged pieces of machinery which should ordinarily last twenty-five years or more. Breakdowns are rare on these units, although beaters may need replacing sooner, depending on the number of spoons you feed to them. The most common affliction in these machines derives from the fact that almost no one ever thinks of oiling her electric mixer! But if you look carefully at the mixer case, you'll find two small holes which ought to be (but aren't) labeled "One or two drops of household oil every six months." You won't detect any difference if you oil regularly, but your mixer will, and its life will be extended.

These mixers are usually equipped with governors so that, regardless of batter thickness, the speed you dial is the speed you get. Occasionally, on older models, these governors stick, and your twelve-speed beater acts as if it can only count to two or three instead of twelve. Cure this problem by unplugging the mixer and then removing the screw that holds the speed control dial in place (it may first be necessary to pry off a stainless steel cover plate that is hiding the screw); next expose the governor mechanism by removing the control dial. It isn't necessary to understand how the governor works; simply spray the whole exposed mechanism lightly with silicone lubricant and reassemble the unit. If you wish to run the mixer with the control dial removed, first check the precautions on page 220.

Should you fail to repair your mixer, don't discard it—it's probably worth professional attention; check your Yellow Pages under "Electrical Appliances, Small—Repairing."

Food mixers, portable: Because, like a hedge clipper, it spends its active life being waved around at the end of its cord, a portable mixer frequently fails because of a wire break where it enters the case. If you can afford to lose 6″ of wire, try cutting that much off at the mixer end and reconnecting. Like their big brothers mentioned above, they often are designed to accept a periodic (twice a year) drop of oil in a small hole in the case at the front end. The back end has no oil hole, but it doesn't hurt to squirt a little silicone lubricant through the ventilation openings while the mixer is running with the back end pointed down.

If the three-speed switch on your mixer fails to give you three speeds, it could be a dirty contact in the switch. Once the case of the mixer is open, you will find it easy to get at these switch contacts with a Q-Tip and alcohol. Many mixers require the additional removal of a screw holding the handle before these contacts are accessible.

Fry pans and griddles, electric: Likely ailments, in order of decreasing probability, are:

(a) A broken cord.

(b) A faulty thermostat switch (see bimetallic strip, page 228).

(c) A burned-out heater element.

If the pilot light fails to light, it's (a) or (b); if you can hear a click of an internal switch as you turn the temperature dial, it's probably (a) or (c). Thus, if you get no pilot light and hear no click, suspect the thermostatic switch; if you hear a click, but see no glow from the pilot light, suspect the cord; if you see a glow, hear a click, but get no heat, suspect the heating element.[1]

---

[1] Unfortunately, a few thermostatically controlled appliances ordinarily turn on and off without clicking; for them this short-cut diagnostic procedure fails.

Replacement of the cord is a routine operation (see page 63), but if the thermostat unit is at fault, you should read page 228 (bimetallic strip), then follow the procedure outlined in chapter 20, page 217.

If your repair effort should fail, and you are fortunate enough to be working with a submersible unit with detachable temperature control, it is definitely worth your while to obtain a replacement temperature control switch from your dealer.

Gas-fired appliances: An automatic, gas-fired appliance, such as a furnace, a hot water heater, or a clothes dryer, has a small flame about one inch high, known as a pilot light, which ignites the main burner when the automatic supply valve opens. The pilot light burns continuously—at least it's supposed to. Pilot lights *do* go out occasionally, however, usually for one of three reasons: a breeze, a temporary break in the gas flow, or a burned-out thermocouple.

A thermocouple is a pencil-shaped (but smaller) electric sensor, directly in the pilot flame and normally so hot it glows red, which signals a gas cut-off should anything happen to the pilot flame. The minute the pilot goes out—zap! the gas to the appliance is automatically cut off. And it can flow normally again only when the pilot is lit again and reheats the thermocouple until it is red hot.

Take a few minutes for a pre-trouble visit to the basement (or wherever your gas appliances are); the time spent may pay royal dividends later. Check whatever gas-fired appliances you own and locate the pilot light. If things are quiet, you'll hear a soft hiss of the flame. (If the big burner of the appliance happens to be on, you will have to wait until it's off to hear the pilot.) You should be able to see the pilot flame easily, though it may be necessary to open a little metal door or remove a snap-on cover at the base of the water heater or on the dryer.

When there's no hot water or you've turned up the thermostat and the house is still cold or when you open the dryer and the clothes, instead of being fluffy and warm, are clammy —there's a better than even chance that the pilot light is out.

If either wind or a temporary interruption of the gas flow was responsible, you can easily and safely relight the pilot. Every gas-fired appliance has a safety gas cut-off activated by a thermocouple.

If gas-fired, your furnace or water heater or clothes dryer each will have a metal plate attached giving specific and easy-to-understand directions for relighting the pilot. Use the directions attached to your particular appliance and follow them exactly.

But suppose you have followed directions—several times— and the pilot still goes out when you release the reset button. Now what? In all probability the thermocouple has given up the ghost; and it's one of those things that has to be replaced —not repaired. This is a job for the gas repairman. With your trouble light in hand, take a hard look at the thermocouple. The entire end may have burned off or there may be a hole in the side, or the damage may be invisible.

Griddles, electric: See Fry pans and griddles, electric.

Hedge clippers, electric: Failure is almost invariably due to a break in the wire where it enters the handle. See page 214 for counsel. Remember to lubricate the cutting blades occasionally.

Mixers, food: See Food mixers, counter-top and Food mixers, portable.

Pilot lights: See Gas-fired appliances.

Sewing machines: If your sewing machine is misbehaving, I'll give you odds that you haven't lubricated it according to the instruction book for over a year. Get out your manual— you'll be surprised to find detailed instructions for the lubrication and maintenance of your machine.

Shavers, battery-powered: See Battery-powered carving knives, toothbrushes, and shavers.

Shavers, line-operated: Failure is usually caused by an invisible break in the cord where it meets the plug that connects to the shaver. The "cord compression trick" shown on page 215 will probably get you through the morning, but a new cord is in order and is available from most appliance dealers. If a new cord does nothing, get your tiniest screwdriver (if you have no screwdriver small enough, a nail file may work) and, after removing the shaver head, open the case of the shaver slowly and carefully, noting the position of all parts as they come into view. Look for a broken wire, a wad of hair jammed around a moving part, or evidence of friction when you rotate the motor. Remembering the precautions cited on page 220, try switching it on with the case open.

Should all your tinkering lead to nothing but silence, you may wish to check the Yellow Pages for Small Appliance Repair—the manufacturer of your shaver may have a repair shop in your city.

If your shaver is running more slowly than it did in days of yore, a shot of spray silicone lubricant on the motor bearings or the cutting head may speed it up dramatically.

Steam irons: Defective cords (and this is the most common problem) on irons are easy to replace, particularly when you take the trouble to get an *exact duplicate* replacement from the hardware store; but woe unto the person who tries to fix much more than that on an iron! Iron manufacturers have consciously designed their product so that it can't be disassembled without damaging one of the parts of the iron. It is argued that this prevents non-experts from ignorantly "repairing" their irons into lethal weapons full of shooting steam, and I'll admit that the argument has validity. But it follows that when your iron acts up in an area other than the cord, it's best to simply buy a new one.

When the manufacturers say that distilled water or deionized water must be used in steam irons, they are telling the truth; if your iron now spits, fumes, and drips instead of hissing politely, because you have used tap water, your best move is to slap your hand, promise yourself to use no more tap water, and start again with a new iron.

Toasters: Toasters are for tinkerers who have autographed portraits of Rube Goldberg over their workbenches. If you have an infinite supply of patience and time, you can almost always figure out and repair the odd assortment of levers, rods, screws, cams, latches, catches, and bimetallic strips. If you enjoy doing thousand-piece jigsaw puzzles, you'll soon be so addicted to tinkering with these devices that you'll be getting up early to raid trash cans in search of old toasters.

Even if you hate puzzles, don't believe in patience, and break out in a rash when you hear the name of Rube Goldberg, you owe it to yourself to take your balky toaster apart just to wiggle the levers and latches. Who knows?—a shot of silicone lubricant, a tightened (or loosened) adjusting screw, or a cleaned up contact may be all it needs!

If you do feel moved to try to understand the soul of your suffering toaster, you will want to know about the bimetallic strip (no, it's not a new dance step!) which activates the automatic pop-up mechanism. The strip actually consists of *two* metal strips of different composition lying face to face, welded together at each end. The metals are chosen so that one of these two strips expands greatly when heated and the other expands hardly at all. The resulting strip starts off straight

... WHEN IT'S COLD:

but it bends more and more as it gets hot, as the length of the two strips

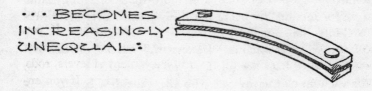

... BECOMES INCREASINGLY UNEQUAL:

Now, if the bimetallic strip is part of an electric circuit, it can, by bending as the current heats it up, act as a switch:

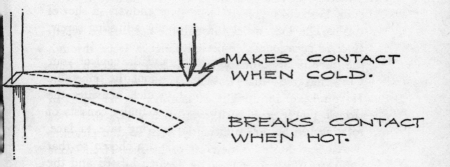

MAKES CONTACT WHEN COLD.

BREAKS CONTACT WHEN HOT.

You'll find at least two of these acting as switches in most automatic toasters; they're often bluish in color. These ingenious strips also show up in virtually all thermostats, from the one on your wall that controls the house temperature to the one on your electric fry pan that allows you to dial its operating temperature.

Vacuum cleaners: If any household appliance is likely to need a psychiatrist, the vacuum cleaner is it. It is easily the most completely misunderstood item in the house. In the same week that thousands of easily repairable vacuum cleaners are being discarded, thousands of other vacuum cleaners that haven't gasped or sucked in more than an emphysemic wheeze for months are being faithfully pushed over dirty rugs by well-intentioned people.

Of course, most vacuum cleaners sniff instead of suck because their dust bags are filled. If you're one of the multitude of the vacuum cleaner owners who allow the dust bag to overfill, put down this book and install a new bag right now. A bag that feels over half full is ready to be retired or emptied. But many vacuums, even after replacement of the bag, will merely whir and wheeze a little for one of a number of reasons:

1. The hose on your canister model may be clogged with your husband's favorite golf ball or your son's lost turtle. The broomstick-through-the-hose test is worth making occasionally, especially once a week through the month of January if you had a Scotch pine Christmas tree—those needles just love to jam!

2. If you have an upright or canister model with an electric power rug brush, even money says that your rotating brushes are sufficiently worn so that cleaning action is reduced. A new set of brushes (from your appliance dealer) is easy to install—usually the removal of a bottom plate is sufficient to allow removal of the rubber drive belt and roller so you can slide out the brushes. Each brush may be held in place by a small screw, and at each end of the roller there may be a little clamp which lifts forward to release the spindle on which the roller turns.

3. In an upright model the round, rubber drive belt from the motor to the blower may be broken. The motor will run merrily along (even faster than usual!) but the cleaner won't pick up one speck of anything because the brushes aren't turning and

there isn't any vacuum. New drive belts are inexpensive, readily available, and easy to install: Turn the cleaner over on its back, remove the roller that holds the brushes (see reason 2. above), and follow the directions imprinted on the metal plate between the motor spindle and the roller area. Takes about two minutes.

4. Many canister models have, in addition to the dust bag, a second filter (usually of felt and wire) which covers the opening to the blower housing. If it's dusty, remove it, close the vacuum cleaner, and vacuum it clean before reinstalling it.

5. Upright and canister vacuum cleaners differ in an important, little appreciated characteristic: the location of the motor blower with respect to the path of the dirt.

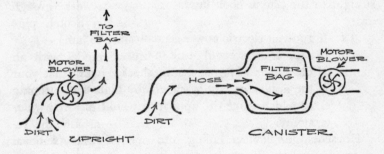

The motor in the canister model enjoys one of the cleanest spots in town, while the upright motor blower lives in the dirtiest spot conceivable. The canister blower simply pulls; the upright blower bats and blows at everything that comes by. The result is twofold: First, the horsepower of the upright motor needs to be only one-third as great as that of the canister model, and, second, the possibility of getting the upright's blower clogged with the hair from your Saint Bernard is pretty high. So if you have an upright that nibbles at dirt as if it just ate dinner somewhere else, try disassembling the blower unit. It's really not hard (easier than a toaster!)— just turn the vacuum upside down and start loosening every screw in sight. It's almost impossible to go wrong in disassembling a vacuum, as long as you remember exactly how things came apart. Check chapter 20, especially pages 217 to 220 for suggestions to make the job easier. Try to follow the air path, pulling the strings and dust from all the nooks and crannies you encounter in your adventure.

But you shouldn't tackle everything: If you have, by now, repaired thirteen lamps, restored the snap in your light switches and the pop in several toasters, rewired your sump pump, and replaced your old toilet, feel free to ignore the advice that follows; but if you are the unconfident novice for whom this book has been designed, take me seriously when I suggest that there are four conditions under which a malfunction should send you straight to the phone book instead of to your toolbox. They are:

1. If 230-volt electric power is involved.
2. If a repair error could result in fire.
3. If the danger of severe electric shock is high.
4. If the appliance cost is sufficiently high that a repair error which ruins the appliance would dislocate your economy.

Household appliances falling into one or more of these categories include the stove, oven, furnace (except for lighting the pilot light), refrigerator, dishwasher, clothes washer (except for replacing broken hoses), clothes dryer (except for lighting the pilot light in gas-fired models), and air conditioner. Trouble in any one of these units is best handled by a trained technician, in spite of his high cost. But, before that technician arrives, read chapter 22!

22

How to Help the Repairman
Avoid Gouging You

Let's face it. You bought this book, not because you were a gung-ho, razzle-dazzle, fix-everything-in-sight person, but because you were somebody who *didn't* enjoy fixing things but weren't exactly wild about your poverty produced by repairmen's bills.

Now you've been through the book. You've knocked off the exercises in chapters 5, 9, and 13. You've bought a few tools, met a few household problems, saved a few dollars.

But I am astute enough to know that when you go to bed at night, you *don't* fall asleep eagerly hoping that some new repair challenge will appear by morning.

Just because you replaced a pane in your cellar window doesn't mean that you want to replace your 4'×7' picture window when your delicate daughter throws her little brother through it (although you may feel, at that point, like replacing your delicate daughter!). You call a glazier.

Just because you replaced the cord on your iron doesn't mean that you are aching to repair your defunct clothes dryer. And the fact that you dared to replace your own toilet seat doesn't make you an aspiring plumber.

You're still you. (Good thing—what a dangerous book this would be if you weren't!) Hopefully a little less helpless, but still possessed of enough caution and good sense not to burn that second little black book—the one with names and phone numbers of the refrigerator man, the washing machine man, the plumber, the electrician, and an auto mechanic or two.

You'll still need repairmen and mechanics, and they'll still charge you plenty. The question is: How do you encourage them to resist the temptation to overcharge you and perform unnecessary jobs for you? And how do you learn as much as possible from them while they're serving you?

Two years ago I would have advised you to learn a little of the jargon and names of the parts of each appliance, and then do a little judicious name dropping. For example, I felt that a useful line to practice on for the washing machine man as you led him toward your machine that had stopped in the middle of its spin cycle would be, "I'm not sure what the problem is—I suppose it could be a clutch, a belt, a solenoid, or even the timer—I just don't know," thereby making clear to him that you know enough and are interested enough to warrant a coherent explanation of the ailment and the cure. And he wouldn't dare tell you he replaced three nonexistent parts, adjusted two nonadjustable switches, checked the frame for strains and examined the floor for levelness for an extra $10.50.

But then a surprising statement by a long-time service manager in a large garage changed my tune considerably. He said, "I think that over the years we have bilked a higher percentage of the men than of women." He went on to explain two reasons for this: First, the man doesn't know anything and is afraid to admit it, so a typical conversation about a car brought in for a tune-up might go like this:

"Sir, your ※1 spark plug wire shows 20,000 ohms resistance!"

"Oh? Why—er—well—I guess you better take care of it, then."

"Shall I replace the entire spark plug harness, sir? The other wires are probably about the same age."

"Uh—Yeah—That's right—Sure, better do it right."

A woman, on the other hand doesn't know anything, and is ready to admit it. With her the conversation would go:

"Ma'am, the wire that goes to your front spark plug reads 20,000 ohms."

"Oh really? Is that bad?"

"Well, it's hard to say, ma'am. It should be about 10,000 ohms."

"But would the car run much better if you fixed it?"

"Well, that's hard to say, ma'am. You might not notice any improvement."

"Well—I guess I'll let it go then until it causes trouble. Just give it a regular tune-up."

That woman just saved herself $20 by being willing to show ignorance.

A second reason is simply that in an auto repair situation, men are fair game because mechanics expect men to be able to fend for themselves, while many mechanics feel that doing the same thing to a woman would obviously be taking advantage of her. This may be a subtle form of male chauvinism, but whatever it is, it's a factor in the formula that decides how you, a woman, can best get maximum value from a service call.

Now, I'll admit that the game of auto repair is different from the game of washing machine repair because of the complexity of the auto, the different criteria of what constitutes "running well," and the obvious attachment that men have for their cars. (Whoever heard of a husband who "took Ed for a spin around the cycles in our new washing machine?") But nevertheless, I've become convinced that there are enough similarities to suggest an approach:

1. Be sufficiently friendly for him to feel chivalrous toward you rather than antagonistic, and watch him while he works.

2. Don't try to act as if you know more than you do.
3. Ask questions.
4. Ask questions.
5. Ask more questions.
6. And more questions—
7. Until you *really do* understand what went wrong.

The real key is in the questions. Start with a couple that establish your respect for his skill and authority:

"Do you think it could be a switch?"

"Does this particular model tend to break down more often than others?"

When he makes his diagnosis, admiringly ask him, "Now how in the world can you tell something like that?"

And his answer will precipitate another question, and you'll be learning. The words to remember are "Why" and "How" and "What":

"What does it mean when you say a bearing is frozen?"

"Why does that jammed bearing stop the machine only on the spin cycle?"

"How did the bearing get that way?"

"Is it quite difficult to replace?"

"How likely is it to happen again?"

"What can I do to prevent a recurrence?"

"How about the other bearings? Are they in good shape?"

Chances are that, as long as that repairman feels important and appreciated, you'll get his best work and unpadded billing —and you'll learn a little for the next time!

I quite confidently predict that each "next time" will be more distant, less frequent, and not so traumatic. For, if you've truly caught the spirit of this book, you'll pick up that screwdriver more and more readily and call for costly repairmen less and less quickly.

And before long you will have discovered for yourself: You really *don't* need a man to fix it!

Index